乘风汉语 1

CHENGO CHINESE

学生用书

Student's Book

教材项目规划小组

许　琳　　马箭飞　　赵　路

陈伟光　　董德刚　　陈希原

赵国成　　宋永波　　郭　鹏

目录

第一集

你 好

第一集 你好

一、课　文

韩　江：你好，陆大伟！

陆大伟：你好，韩江！

跑步人：你好！脸谱！

陆大伟：你好，脸谱！

骑车人：你好！脸谱！

陆大伟：你好，脸谱！

王子欣：你好！

陆大伟：你好，脸谱！我是陆大伟。

王子欣：我是王子欣，很高兴认识你。

陆大伟：你好，脸谱，韩江！

韩　江：你好，陆大伟！

陆大伟：这是王子欣。

韩　江：你好，王子欣！很高兴认识你。

王子欣：你好，韩江！很高兴认识你。

Hán Jiāng: Nǐ hǎo, Lù Dàwěi!
Lù Dàwěi: Nǐ hǎo, Hán Jiāng!
Pǎobùrén: Nǐ hǎo! Liǎnpǔ!
Lù Dàwěi: Nǐ hǎo, liǎnpǔ!
Qíchērén: Nǐ hǎo! Liǎnpǔ!
Lù Dàwěi: Nǐ hǎo, liǎnpǔ!

Wáng Zǐxīn: Nǐ hǎo!
Lù Dàwěi: Nǐ hǎo, liǎnpǔ! Wǒ shì Lù Dàwěi.
Wáng Zǐxīn: Wǒ shì Wáng Zǐxīn, hěn gāoxìng rènshi nǐ.
Lù Dàwěi: Nǐ hǎo, liǎn pǔ, Hán Jiāng!
Hán Jiāng: Nǐ hǎo, Lù Dàwěi!
Lù Dàwěi: Zhè shì Wáng Zǐxīn.
Hán Jiāng: Nǐ hǎo, Wáng Zǐxīn! Hěn gāoxìng rènshi nǐ.
Wáng Zǐxīn: Nǐ hǎo, Hán Jiāng! Hěn gāoxìng rènshi nǐ.

John: Hello, David.
David: Hello, John.
Runner: Hello! Lianpu.
David: Hello, lianpu.
Biker: Hello! Lianpu.
David: Hello, lianpu.

Cindy: Hello!
David: Hello, lianpu. I'm David Lumley.
Cindy: I'm Cindy Wang. Nice to meet you.
David: Hello, lianpu, John.
John: Hello, David.
David: This is Cindy Wang.
John: Hello, Cindy. I'm glad to meet you.
Cindy: Hello, John. Glad to meet you.

韩　江：你好，老师马！啊，对不起对不起，马老师。

马老师：你好，韩江！

王子欣：马老师好！我是王子欣，很高兴认识马老师。

陆大伟：马老师，你好，脸谱！

马老师：脸谱？这是脸谱。

陆大伟：什么？

马老师：这是脸谱！

陆大伟：啊，你是脸谱！

王子欣：你好，脸谱！我是王子欣，很高兴认识你！

Hán Jiāng :	Nǐ hǎo, lǎoshī Mǎ! À, duìbuqǐ duìbuqǐ, Mǎ lǎoshī.
Mǎ Lǎoshī :	Nǐ hǎo, Hán Jiāng.
Wáng Zǐxīn :	Mǎ lǎoshī hǎo! Wǒ shì Wáng Zǐxīn, hěn gāoxìng rènshi Mǎ lǎoshī.
Lù Dàwěi :	Mǎ lǎoshī, nǐ hǎo, liǎnpǔ!
Mǎ Lǎoshī :	Liǎnpǔ? Zhè shì liǎnpǔ.
Lù Dàwěi :	Shénme?
Mǎ Lǎoshī :	Zhè shì liǎnpǔ!
Lù Dàwěi :	Á, nǐ shì liǎnpǔ!
Wáng Zǐxīn:	Nǐ hǎo, liǎnpǔ! Wǒ shì Wáng Zǐxīn, hěn gāoxìng rènshi nǐ!

John:	Hello, laoshi Ma. Oh, I'm sorry, Ma laoshi.
Teacher Ma:	Hello, John.
Cindy:	Hello, Teacher Ma. I'm Cindy Wang. I'm glad to meet you, Teacher Ma.
David:	Teacher Ma, how are you, lianpu?
Teacher Ma:	Lianpu? This is a lianpu.
David:	What?
Teacher Ma:	This is a lianpu.
David:	Oh, you're a lianpu.
Cindy:	Lianpu, how are you? I'm Cindy. It is nice to meet you!

1. 你	nǐ	you
2. 好	hǎo	good; fine
3. 脸谱	liǎnpǔ	lianpu,Chinese opera makeup
4. 我	wǒ	I; me
5. 是	shì	to be (is, am, are)
6. 很	hěn	very; quite
7. 高兴	gāoxìng	happy; glad
8. 认识	rènshi	to know; to recognize
9. 老师	lǎoshī	teacher
10. 马	mǎ	Ma, a surname; horse
11. 对不起	duìbuqǐ	sorry; Excuse me!
12. 这	zhè	this
13. 什么	shénme	what
14. 啊 *	à	ah, oh (used to express sudden realization or admiration)
15. 啊 *	á	ah, oh (used to express surprise)

The symbol * indicates that the corresponding word is not practiced in this episode.

三、语言注释

你好

你好 is the most common way for greeting people in Chinese. It can be used when you meet someone for the first time, or between acquaintances, in both formal and informal situations.

马老师

When you address someone by his/her title or occupation in Chinese, make sure to say that person's surname before his/her title or occupation. e.g.

张教授
Professor Zhang

王大夫
Doctor Wang

陆先生
Mr. Lu

王小姐
Miss Wang

老 lǎo

古文字中，“老”象一个留着长发、弯腰弓背、手拄拐杖的老人。“老”本义就是年纪大，现在人们还称年迈的父母为“二老”。

中国自古就有尊敬老人的习惯，因而“老”可用作尊称，如对某些有一定地位和影响的老人，可称“李老、王老”。后来凡是历时长久的人、东西都可称老，如“老朋友、老电影”。

“老”还可以用作词缀，如“老师、老虎”。

In ancient Chinese script, the character 老 resembles a longhaired old man stooping over with a bent back while holding a cane in one hand. The original meaning of 老 is advanced in years or elderly. Nowadays, Chinese people still often refer to their elderly parents as 二老 (father and mother). From ancient times, Chinese people have followed a custom of showing great respect toward elders. For this reason, 老 can also be used as a term of respect. For example, elderly people of a certain status or influence may be referred to as 李老 (Honourable Mr. Li) or 王老 (Esteemed Madam Wang), etc. With the passing of time, any person or thing with a long history also could be referred to as 老 (old). For example, in Chinese you can say 老电影 (old movie) or 老朋友 (old friend). 老 can also be used as a prefix for nouns such as: 老师 (teacher) or 老虎 (tiger).

好 hǎo

古文字中，“好”的左边是“女”，右边是“子”，意思是“女子貌美”。现在有的方言称赞一个人长得漂亮也还说“某某人长得好”。后来凡是美的、善的、优秀的，都可以说“好”，如“好人、好东西、好喝”。

In ancient Chinese, the character 好, which is made up of 女 on the left, and 子 on the right, meant “an attractive woman”. Nowadays, in some Chinese dialects, people will still say someone looks 好 to mean "handsome" or "beautiful". Later, 好 came to be used to refer to anything beautiful, kind, or outstanding. For example, the word can be used in：好人 (good person), 好东西 (something useful or valuable; good stuff), or 好喝 (nice to drink).

高 gāo

古文字中，"高"象人类在高地上建的穴居之形。

人类穴居一般都选择地势高的地方，"高"的本义就是从下至上距离大、离地面远（与"低"相对），如"弟弟很高、高山"。后来，凡是在一般标准或平均程度之上的，都可以说"高"，如"高温、高速度"等。

Originally, 高 was a pictographic character in ancient Chinese resembling the shape of a man-made cave dwelling built on a highland or plateau. Throughout history, people generally have chosen to build cave-dwellings on elevated terrain. The original meaning of 高 was at a great distance from bottom to top or far off the ground (In Chinese, its opposite is 低 (low)). For example, 弟弟很高 (Younger brother is quite tall.) or 高山 (high mountain). Eventually, anything higher than the average degree or usual standard could also be described as 高, for example, 高温 (high temperature(s)), 高速度 (high speed), etc.

你	你	你	你	你	你	你	你			
好	好	好	好	好	好	好				
老	老	老	老	老	老	老				
师	师	师	师	师	师	师				

中国人的姓名　Chinese Names

中国人的名字分为姓和名两部分，姓在前，名在后，排列与英语相反。比如，王冰。用拼音拼写时，姓和名要分写，姓和名的第一个字母要大写，比如 Wang Bing。

子女一般都用父亲的姓，妇女婚嫁后一般保持本姓。

取名时，通常都喜欢给自己或者子女选择一个好听的、意义美好的名字。

▶ 相关信息

姓有一个字的单姓，也有两个字或两个字以上的复姓，如“公孙、司马”等。

取名时要尽量避免与父母或其他长辈重名，因为中国传统文化崇尚敬老，一般不直接称呼父母、长辈、老师的名。

中国历史上共有姓近12000个，现在常用的只有200个左右。比如，张、王、李、赵、刘、马、陆、韩等。

Most Chinese names are usually made up of two parts: a surname and a given name. In contrast to English names, the surname precedes the given name, as in “Wang Bing”. When spelt in Pinyin (the Chinese Phonetic Script), the surname and the given name should be separated by a space, with the first letter of each capitalized.

Although children generally take their father’s surname in China, Chinese women usually keep their own surname after marriage.

Chinese normally like to give themselves or their children beautiful personal names which sound pleasant and convey positive or favorable symbolic meanings.

▶ [Additional Notes]

Most Han Chinese surnames have only one character, but there are a few compound surnames consisting of two characters such as Gongsun and Sima.

Children’s names should not be the same as their parents or other elder family members in accordance with the Chinese traditional value of showing respect toward the aged. For the same reason, parents, elders, people in higher positions and teachers should not be addressed directly by their given names.

As many as 12, 000 surnames have been recorded in Chinese history, but only some 200 remain in common use today, such as Zhang, Wang, Li, Zhao, Liu, Ma, Lu, Han, etc.

关于“老师” “Laoshi” as a Form of Address

汉语用“姓＋老师”来称呼学校里的教师，表示礼貌和尊敬，如“马老师、张老师”。不管是小学还是中学、大学，甚至幼儿园，都可以使用“老师”一词。

不过，“老师”一词不只局限于教师的范围。比如，在学校办公室工作的人也被称为“老师”，文艺圈中有时称一些年长的人为“老师”。这种情况下，“老师”已经成为一个表示礼貌的敬称，跟对方的职业无关。中国素有“尊师重教”的传统，用“老师”一词称呼某方面值得学习的人，显得谦逊有礼。

In Chinese, schoolteachers are generally addressed by their surnames and the term “Laoshi” is added after their surnames to show courtesy and respect, as in “Ma Laoshi” and “Zhang Laoshi”. “Laoshi” can be used to address educators from kindergarten teachers to university professors.

Nowadays, however, “Laoshi” is used as a form of address not only for teachers, but also for staff members in school offices, and for distinguished artists and writers. In this regard, “Laoshi” may also be used as a term of respect or a polite form of address which has nothing to do with the professions of the people being addressed to. As China has a long tradition of honoring teachers and revering their teachings, it is considered a polite way of showing respect to address someone from whom we can learn something as “Laoshi”.

自我介绍 Introducing Oneself

在社交场合初次见面时，通常要先跟对方打招呼，然后再自我介绍。介绍时可以只说出自己的姓，也可以说出姓和名，还可以告诉对方自己的身份。比如：“你好，我姓马，是北京大学的老师。”或“您好，我是王冰，北京大学的学生。”

有时候你认识对方，但对方却不认识你。这个时候，你可以说：“您是马老师吧？我是陆大伟，美国留学生。”

▶ **相关信息**

中国人在自我介绍时，一般只介绍自己的姓名以及工作，不大愿意主动介绍自己的职务或职称。在正式场合，可以通过名片表明自己的职务或职称。给长辈递名片时，一般要用双手，以示尊敬。

正式场合自我介绍以后，传统的方法是双方鞠躬或者作揖，现代的方法是互相握手。

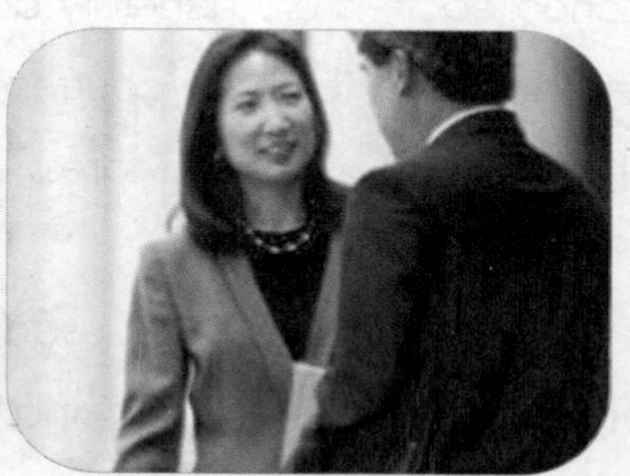

When two people meet for the first time during social occasions, it is customary for them to make a self-introduction immediately after greeting each other. During the introduction, either the surname or full name is usually mentioned while other personal information may also be included. e.g.

你好，我姓马，是北京大学的老师。(Literally means: Hello, my surname is Ma, a teacher from Peking University.)

您好，我是王冰，北京大学的学生。(Literally means: Hello, I am Wang Bing, a student from Peking University.)

Sometimes you know someone who may not know you. In this case you can say, “You are Ma Laoshi, aren't you? I am Lu Dawei, an international student from the U.S.”

[Additional Notes]

When Chinese make self-introductions, they usually mention their names and careers only. Positions or titles are rarely included. On some formal occasions, one can present a business card with one's position or academic titles. When giving a card to a person of a senior social position, you should hold it with both hands to show respect.

Traditionally, a formal self-introduction is usually followed by a bow. Nowadays, however, a handshake or a handshake and a nod are common.

脸谱 Chinese Opera Makeup

脸谱是戏曲中某些角色脸上画的各种图案，用来表示人物的性格和特征，充满着浓厚的道德评价色彩。和面具不同，脸谱直接画在脸上。中国传统戏曲都有脸谱艺术，京剧脸谱是它们的代表。

相关信息

一般用黑、红、白、黄、绿、蓝等颜料涂满整张脸，特别突出眉、眼、鼻、口等部位。不同颜色，以及眉、眼、鼻、口的不同画法，代表不同的意义。比如在京剧中，红色的脸谱表示忠诚勇敢，黑色的脸谱表示正直勇猛，黄色的脸谱表示凶狠残暴，蓝色或绿色表示刚强猛烈，性格暴躁，白色一般代表有严重缺陷的人，或者是阴险毒辣的坏人。紫色表示刚正耿直，金色和银色基本上用于神仙妖怪一类的角色。

Chinese opera makeup (lianpu in Chinese) refers to the various patterns on the faces of actors and actresses in operas to indicate different personalities and characters of different roles, as well as to express moral judgment and appraisal of these characters. Unlike masks, all of the various lianpu patterns are directly painted on the actors' faces. Traditional Chinese opera makes wide use of the art of facial makeup and Beijing Opera makeup is the most representative form of this technique.

[Additional Notes]

It is common to use black, red, white, yellow, green, and blue makeup to paint the entire face of traditional opera actors. Certain parts of the face such as the eyebrows, eyes, nose, and mouth are highlighted. Different facial makeup patterns hold different meanings, depending on the colors used and the way in which highlighted areas are painted. In Beijing Opera, for instance, a red face symbolizes loyalty and bravery; a black face denotes righteousness and valor; a yellow face indicates cruelty and harshness; a blue or green face demonstrates toughness, fierceness and a hot-temper; a white face is used for underhanded or crafty villains; a purple face represents integrity; while gold or silver faces usually represent monsters or gods.

六、场景探索

场景一

1. 房子 fángzi house
2. 树 shù tree
3. 汽车 qìchē bus
4. 草地 cǎodì grassy area
5. 湖 hú lake
6. 山 shān mountain
7. 邮筒 yóutǒng mailbox
8. 椅子 yǐzi chair
9. 秋千 qiūqiān swing

场景二

1. 桌子 zhuōzi desk
2. 椅子 yǐzi chair
3. 地球仪 dìqiúyí globe
4. 花 huā flower
5. 天坛 tiāntán the Temple of Heaven
6. 对联 duìlián a pair of scrolls containing a poetic couplet
7. 地图 dìtú map
8. 书 shū book
9. 门 mén door

第二集

这是什么

第二集　这是什么

一、课 文

韩　江：大家看，长城！

马老师：对，这是长城。

王子欣：长城真漂亮！

陆大伟：马老师，这是熊猫吗？

马老师：对，这是熊猫。

王子欣：熊猫真可爱！

马老师：这是孔子。你们知道他吗？

韩　江：我不知道。

王子欣：我知道，他是老师。

韩　江：他是老师，你也是老师。

马老师：他是有名的老师，我不是！

⊙	Hán Jiāng:	Dàjiā kàn, Chángchéng!
	Mǎ Lǎoshī:	Duì, zhè shì Chángchéng.
	Wáng Zǐxīn:	Chángchéng zhēn piàoliang!
⊙	Lù Dàwěi:	Mǎ lǎoshī, zhè shì xióngmāo ma?
	Mǎ Lǎoshī:	Duì, zhè shì xióngmāo.
	Wáng Zǐxīn:	Xióngmāo zhēn kě'ài!
⊙	Mǎ Lǎoshī:	Zhè shì Kǒngzǐ. Nǐmen zhīdào tā ma?
	Hán Jiāng:	Wǒ bù zhīdào.
	Wáng Zǐxīn:	Wǒ zhīdào, tā shì lǎoshī.
	Hán Jiāng:	Tā shì lǎoshī, nǐ yě shì lǎoshī.
	Mǎ Lǎoshī:	Tā shì yǒumíng de lǎoshī, wǒ bú shì!
⊙	John:	Look, everyone. The Great Wall!
	Teacher Ma:	Right. This is the Great Wall.
	Cindy:	The Great Wall is really beautiful!
⊙	David:	Teacher Ma, is this a panda?
	Teacher Ma:	Yes. This is a panda.
	Cindy:	Pandas are so cute.
⊙	Teacher Ma:	This is Confucius. Do you know who he was?
	John:	I don't know.
	Cindy:	I know. He was a teacher.
	John:	He was a teacher. You're a teacher, too.
	Teacher Ma:	He was a famous teacher. I'm not.

⊙ 陆大伟：我知道，这是姚明！

王子欣：我也知道！姚明真酷！

韩　江：姚明，你好！我是韩江，很高兴认识你！

⊙ 马老师：大家看，这是什么？

陆大伟：我知道，这是画。

王子欣：不，这是字。

马老师：对，这是字，不是画。

陆大伟：啊，是字，是什么字？

马老师：是“马”字。马老师，“马”。

Lù Dàwěi: Wǒ zhīdào, zhè shì Yáo Míng!

Wáng Zǐxīn: Wǒ yě zhīdào! Yáo Míng zhēn kù!

Hán Jiāng: Yáo Míng, nǐ hǎo! Wǒ shì Hán Jiāng, hěn gāoxìng rènshi nǐ!

Mǎ Lǎoshī: Dàjiā kàn, zhè shì shénme?

Lù Dàwěi: Wǒ zhīdào, zhè shì huà.

Wáng Zǐxīn: Bù, zhè shì zì.

Mǎ Lǎoshī: Duì, zhè shì zì, bú shì huà.

Lù Dàwěi: Á, shì zì, shì shénme zì?

Mǎ Lǎoshī: Shì “mǎ” zì. Mǎ lǎoshī, “mǎ”.

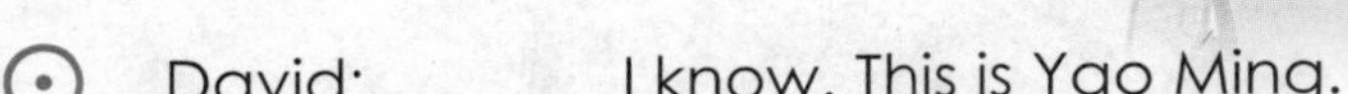

David: I know. This is Yao Ming.

Cindy: So do I. Yao Ming is really cool!

John: How do you do, Yao Ming? I’ m John Hanks. I’ m very glad to meet you!

Teacher Ma: Look, everyone. What is this?

David: I know. This is a painting.

Cindy: No. This is a character.

Teacher Ma: Yes. This is a character, not a painting.

David: Oh, it’ s a character. What character is this?

Teacher Ma: It is the character for “Ma” , the “Ma” in Teacher Ma.

二、词语表

1. 大家	dàjiā	everybody
2. 长城	Chángchéng	the Great Wall
3. 对	duì	right; correct
4. 真	zhēn	very; really; so
5. 漂亮	piàoliang	beautiful; pretty
6. 熊猫	xióngmāo	panda
7. 吗	ma	particle (used at the end of a question)
8. 可爱	kě'ài	cute; lovely; lovable
9. 知道	zhīdào	to know
10. 他	tā	he; him
11. 不	bù	not; no
12. 也	yě	also; too
13. 酷	kù	cool
14. 画	huà	drawing; painting
15. 啊	á	ah; oh
16. 字	zì	character
17. 看 *	kàn	to look at; to watch; to see
18. 孔子 *	Kǒngzǐ	Confucius
19. 有名 *	yǒumíng	famous; well known
20. 的 *	de	particle (used after an attributive)
21. 姚明 *	Yáo Míng	Yao Ming

The symbol * indicates that the corresponding word is not practiced in this episode.

三、语言注释

也

The use of 也 is fairly straightforward. What is important to remember, however, is to always place 也 before verbs. e.g.

马老师是老师，孔子也是老师。

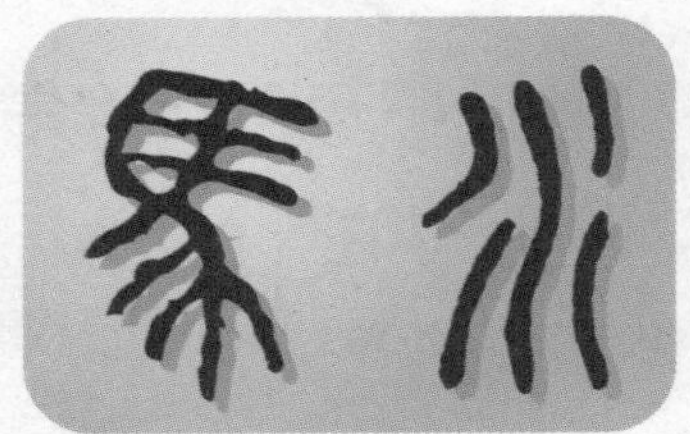

这是字，这也是字。

这是长城，这也是长城。

吗 & 什么

You can use either 吗 or 什么 to make questions. However, 吗 is never used together with 什么! Another point you should also keep in mind is that the word order for interrogative and the declarative sentences is the same in Chinese. e.g.

这是脸谱吗？

这是什么？

A：他是姚明吗？

B：对，他是姚明。

A：这是什么？

B：这是熊猫。

四、汉 字

字 zì

古文字中，“字”的意思是生育。“生育”与汉字有什么关系呢？

传说汉字是黄帝的史官仓颉造出来的。文献上说，仓颉造字的时候，“天雨粟，鬼夜哭”，把汉字的出现看作是一件惊天地、泣鬼神的大事。仓颉造出来的字有两种：一种是不能再进一步拆分的独体字，叫做“文”，如日、月、水等；另一种是用两个或两个以上的“文”组合成的合体字，叫做“字”。之所以叫“字”，是因为它们是由“文”繁衍而来，就如同母体生育孩子一样。

In ancient written Chinese 字 means bear or give birth. So what, then, does “giving birth” have to do with Chinese characters?

According to legend, Chinese characters were invented by the Yellow Emperor's historiographer, Cang Jie. In written records, it is said that when Cang Jie created Chinese characters, “Millet rained down from the sky and demons cried through the night.” The creation of Chinese characters was said to be so momentous as to shake heaven and earth and cause the gods and the spirits to weep. As the legend goes, Cang Jie invented two types of characters: one type was simple characters called 文, which cannot be reduced to smaller units, such as 日, 月 and 水, etc. The second type of characters was the compound character, made by combining two or more simple characters, called 字. The reason compound characters are called 字 is because they are all derived from 文, just as an infant is born of its mother.

画 huà

“画”的繁体字是“畫”，古文字中，“画”上面像一只手拿着笔，下面则是所画出来的图案。“画”的本义就绘画、描画。“画”还可以作名词，意思是图画，如“中国画、油画”。

In classical character form the character 画 is written like 畫. In its ancient form, the character 画 resembles a hand on top with a design or pattern underneath it. The original meaning of 画 is draw or paint. 画 can also denote the noun 图画 (picture; drawing; painting), as in 中国画 (traditional Chinese painting), 油画 (oil painting), or 年画 (spring festival pictures).

城 chéng

古文字中，“城”左边像城墙之形，右边是兵器，表示“守卫”之意。

古代城墙根据建筑材料的不同，可分为土城、石城、砖城。一般来说土城多是古城。现在北京还保留了一段元代土城的遗址。“万里长城”就是长达万里的城墙。

因为古代的“城镇”都有城墙围着，并有士兵防卫。因此，“城”在古代也可以指“城市”，这后来成了“城”的常用义。

In ancient script, the left half of the character 城 resembles the shape of a city wall while the right half represents a weapon; thus the character 城 means 守卫 (safeguard; protect). Ancient city walls can be divided into earthen, stone, and brick city walls, according to the materials used in their construction. Generally speaking, most earthen city walls are more ancient. One section of a Yuan Dynasty (1271 – 1368 A.D.) earthen city wall is still preserved at a site in present-day Beijing. The Great Wall of China or 万里长城 (the ten thousand li Great Wall) is a protective wall which once spanned ten thousand li or approximately five thousand kilometres in length.

Ancient cities and towns were all surrounded by city walls and defended by soldiers. Thus, 城 was also used to indicate 城市 (city) in ancient times and later came to represent its most common meaning.

这

也

不

是

字

介绍他人 Introducing Others

在正式场合，介绍人一般要把被介绍双方的姓名、职务、国籍或身份交代清楚，而且用词也比较礼貌。比如“这位是约翰·史密斯教授，这位是我们学院的院长李新女士。”在一般场合，也可以只介绍姓和职务，比如“这位是李院长。”

在介绍自己的朋友或亲属时，一般要说清楚所介绍的双方与自己的关系，但可以不说亲属的名字。比如把老师介绍给父亲：“爸爸，这是我的汉语老师马老师。马老师，这是我父亲。”

相关信息

介绍时一般先将年长者、职位高的、女士介绍给年轻人、职位低的、男士。介绍完，后者一般应该主动向前者打招呼，说“你好！”

介绍他人互相认识时，介绍人和被介绍的双方通常都应该站立起来，以示礼貌。正式场合介绍完后，如果长辈、上级或女士先伸手，晚辈、下级或男士一般就可以轻轻握一下对方的手；如果他们不主动伸手，一般可以点头微笑致意，或者稍微弯腰鞠躬表示礼貌。

On formal occasions, the person making introductions should clearly and politely state the names, positions, and nationalities of both sides. For example, “This is Professor John Smith. This is Ms. Li Xin, Dean of our department.” In ordinary situations, we generally only introduce people by their surnames and titles. For example, “This is Dean Li.”

When introducing friends or relatives to others, you should give clear information about their relationship with you, but you can leave out their given names. If someone introduces their teacher to their parents, for example, they would likely say, “Dad, this is Ma Laoshi, my Chinese teacher. Ma Laoshi, this is my father.”

▶[Additional Notes]

Elders or people in higher positions, ladies, and dignitaries are usually introduced first. Introductions are then followed by the greeting "Nǐ hǎo" (Hello!) from younger people, men, and people in lower positions.

When introducing people to each other, the person doing the introductions, as well as the people being introduced, should all stand up to show politeness. In formal situations, a handshake, but not too firm, is necessary if elders, superiors, or ladies first extend their hands to younger persons, subordinates or men. If they do not offer to shake hands, one can simply nod and smile or give a slight bow to show courtesy.

长城 The Great Wall

长城始建于公元前七世纪至三世纪的春秋战国时代。当时，诸侯列国为了防御的需要纷纷修建起了长城。秦始皇统一诸侯六国后，把各国长城连接起来，绵延万余里，这就是"万里长城"名字的由来。秦以后，历代不断维修扩建。明代（公元1368—1644年）修建的长城共有7300多公里，西起甘肃嘉峪关，东至河北秦皇岛的山海关。今天我们所见到的主要是明长城。

▶相关信息

长城是中国古代伟大的军事建筑，被誉为古代人类建筑史上的一大奇迹，同时也是世界七大奇迹之一。长城于1987年被联合国世界遗产组织列入《世界遗产名录》，1988年1月被联合国教科文组织列为世界重点历史文物。

万里长城壮观、雄伟，是中华民族智慧的结晶，也是悠久历史的象征。和长城有关的名诗佳作、民间故事历代流传。如今，八达岭、慕田峪、山海关、居庸关、嘉峪关等处经过修复和开发，已经成为驰名中外的旅游胜地，具有极高的旅游观光价值和历史文化意义。

The Great Wall was built between the 7th and 3rd centuries B.C. during the Spring and Autumn Period and the Warring States Period in Chinese history when many states set up walls to defend their territories. After the unification of the six other states by the First Emperor of Qin Dynasty, the various sections of the walls were joined and extended as far as ten thousand li (a traditional unit of length equal to 500 meters), hence taking the name the "Ten-thousand-Li Great Wall" . After the Qin Dynasty, the Great Wall went through constant extensions and repairs in later dynasties. During the Ming Dynasty (1368-1644 A.D.), the entire construction of the walls covered a distance of approximately 7, 300 kilometers, starting from Jiayu Pass in Gansu Province in the west and ending at Shanhai Pass in Hebei Province in the east. The Great Wall we see today was mainly reconstructed during the Ming Dynasty.

▶ **[Additional Notes]**

The Great Wall stands as a magnificent ancient Chinese military structure and is considered an extraordinary feat in the history of ancient architecture. At the same time, it is also regarded as one of the Seven Wonders of the World. In 1987, the World Heritage Committee of UNESCO placed it on the UNESCO World Heritage List. In January 1988, UNESCO further designated it as a major world heritage site of cultural and historical value.

The magnificent Great Wall represents the fruits of the collective wisdom of the Chinese Nation and is symbolic of her long history. Many famous poems and folk stories related to the Great Wall have been handed down through the generations. After further renovation and development, certain sections of the Great Wall such as Badaling, Mutianyu, Shanhai Pass, Juyong Pass and Jiayu Pass have now become famous tourist sites of historical and cultural significance highly praised by travelers, both at home and abroad.

熊猫　Panda

熊猫，又称大熊猫，是世界上最珍贵的动物之一。它身体胖软，头圆颈粗，耳小尾短，四肢粗壮，身长约1.5米，体重可达100—180千克。大熊猫喜爱食竹，不惧严寒，主要分布在中国的四川、甘肃、陕西省的个别崇山峻岭地区，属于国家一级保护动物，称为“国宝”。

▶ **相关信息**

熊猫象征着友谊、和平。中国政府多次将熊猫作为“国礼”赠送给美国人民。它们分别生活在美国亚特兰大、华盛顿、圣地亚哥等城市的动物园，受到了美国人民的喜爱。

为了拯救和保护大熊猫，中国政府采取了一系列有效的措施。至今，四川、甘肃、陕西3省已经建立了多个以保护大熊猫为主的自然保护区。中国政府还在《宪法》中规定大熊猫为国家珍贵保护动物，严厉打击对大熊猫的捕杀。

The panda bear, also known as the giant panda, is one of the most endangered species in the world. It is plump, round-headed and short-necked, with small ears, powerful limbs, and a short tail. It grows to about 1.5 meters in length and usually weighs between 50 to 100 kilograms, but may weigh as much as 180 kilograms. Mainly living in certain mountainous areas of Sichuan, Gansu and Shaanxi Provinces, pandas are fond of eating bamboo and are able to withstand cold temperatures. The giant panda is classified as a level one state-protected animal, and is often referred to as a “national treasure” in China.

▶ **[Additional Notes]**

Pandas have also become Chinese ambassadors of peace and friendship. The Chinese government has donated several pandas as “national gifts” to the American people. They are now living in zoos in Atlanta, Washington and San Diego, and enjoy a great deal of popularity with Americans.

The government protects rare animals in accordance with China's constitution. The Chinese government has also designated the giant panda as an endangered species under state protection and strictly forbids the hunting and killing of pandas. The Chinese government has adopted numerous effective measures in order to protect and save giant pandas from extinction. To date, several nature reserves have been established especially for the protection of pandas in Sichuan, Gansu and Shaanxi Provinces.

孔子 Confucius

孔子（公元前551—公元前479），名丘，字仲尼。春秋末期鲁国陬邑（今山东曲阜东南）人，是中国历史上著名的思想家、政治家、教育家，儒学学派的创始人。

孔子的思想核心是“仁”，也就是“爱人”，主张“己所不欲，毋施于人”。他把“仁”作为行为的规范和目的。

相关信息

孔子一生教过3000多名学生，其中最优秀的有72人。在教学实践中，他总结出一整套教育理论，如因材施教、学思并重、举一反三、启发诱导等教学原则和学而不厌、诲人不倦的教学精神，至今对中国的教育和中国人的思想仍然有着巨大影响。孔子一生的主要言行，被他的学生们记录下来，整理编成《论语》一书，成为后世儒家学派的经典著作。

Confucius (551 B.C.-479 B.C.) named Kong Qiu in Chinese and bearing the style name Zhongni, was born in Zouyi, in the State of Lu (now known as Qufu in southeastern Shandong Province), in the latter part of the Spring and Autumn Period. He is known as the founder of Confucianism and as a famous thinker, statesman, and educator in ancient China.

The core belief of Confucian thought is “humanity” or “love for one’s fellow man”. Confucius maintained that “one should not impose onto others what one does not want to have done onto himself” and set “humanity” as the basis for the rules and aims of personal conduct.

[Additional Notes]

Confucius taught more than 3,000 students in his lifetime, of which, 72 became outstanding scholars. Based on his teaching practice, Confucius summarized a set of educational principles and teaching methods. Examples include: “teaching students according to their aptitude, disposition, and interests" ; "attaching equal importance to learning and reflection" ; "drawing inferences about other cases from one instance" ; and " teaching by elicitation and induction" . He also emphasized that educators should be " insatiable in learning" and "tireless in teaching" . These ideas still have a profound impact on Chinese educational theory and the thinking of Chinese people even today. The main words and deeds of Confucius were recorded and compiled into "The Confucian Analects" by his disciples, which later came to be known as the definitive classic of Confucianism.

姚明 Yao Ming

姚明，1980年9月12日出生，籍贯上海，篮球运动员，绰号"小巨人"。身高2.26米，体重约134公斤。现效力于美国休斯顿火箭队（11号），中国队（13号）。场上位置为中锋。

▶ 相关信息

1997年，获亚洲青年男子篮球锦标赛冠军。1998年，入选中国篮球明星队。2000年2月，入选1999年亚洲全明星队。2002年，当选NBA状元秀，是NBA历史上首位获得"状元秀"的外籍球员。2003年2月，入选 NBA 全明星阵容。

Yao Ming, a famous basketball player with the nickname "Little Giant" , was born in Shanghai on September 12th, 1980. He is 2.26 meters tall and weighs about 134 kilograms. Currently he plays for the Houston Rockets (as No.11) and on the Chinese National Team (as No.13). His court position is center.

▶ **[Additional Notes]**

Yao Ming was awarded MVP status during the 1997 Asian Basketball Championship and was selected to play on the Chinese All-Star Basketball Team in 1998. In February 2000, he was named to the 1999 Asian All-Star Team. In 2002, he was selected to Houston Rockets in the first overall selection in the NBA draft pick and was by then the first foreign super star player in NBA history. In February of 2003, he was chosen to play on the NBA All-Star Team.

象形文字 Chinese Characters as Pictographs

象形文字是描摹实物形状的文字，大多模拟描绘自然界的各种形象。能用象形文字来表示的大部分是名词，如：水、火、羊、月、日、目、马等字。现代汉字是在象形文字的基础上发展起来的。

▶ **相关信息**

汉字自产生至今，经历了长时期的形体演变，总体趋势是由复杂到简单，其大致的发展过程是：甲骨文—金文—篆书—隶书—楷书。如下图中“日、月、云、雨”等字的演变过程。从隶书开始，汉字基本摆脱了象形的特点。

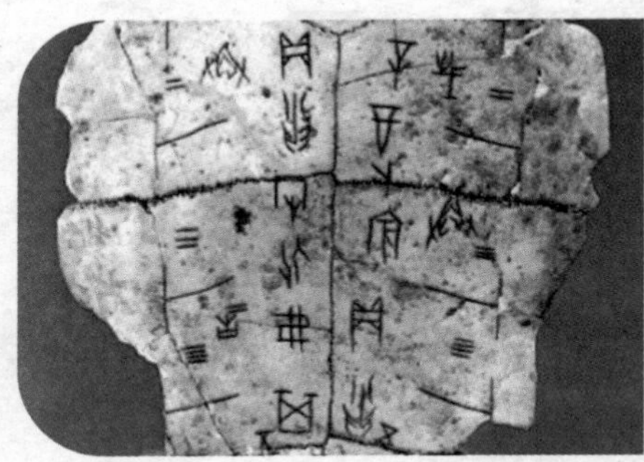

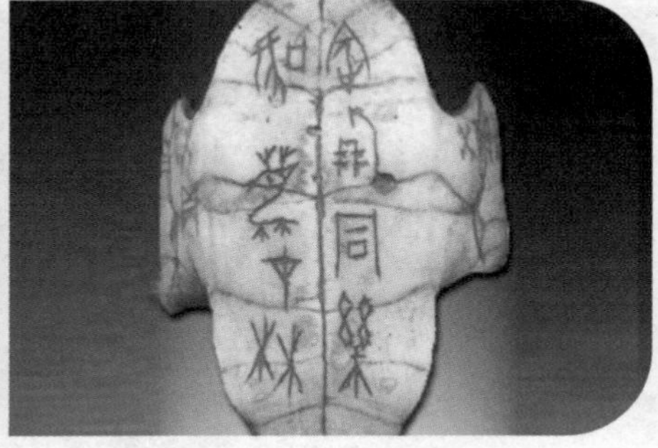

Pictographic characters represent material objects in pictorial form. Most of them are imitations of images in the real world. Modern Chinese characters have evolved from pictographs. Most Chinese pictographic characters are nouns, such as shuǐ (water), huǒ (fire), yáng (sheep), yuè (moon), rì (sun), mù (eye), and mǎ (horse).

▶ **[Additional Notes]**

The form and structure of Chinese characters have undergone continuous development ever since they first came into being at least four or five thousand years ago. The general trend of their development has been one of simplification. Some major stages in this evolutionary process include bone or tortoise shell inscription, ancient bronzeware inscription, seal script, official script, and regular script character forms. From the official script period onward, Chinese characters became more abstract and stylized, hence losing most of their pictographic features. Note the development processes of rì (sun), yuè (moon), yún (cloud) and yǔ (rain) in the following illustrations:

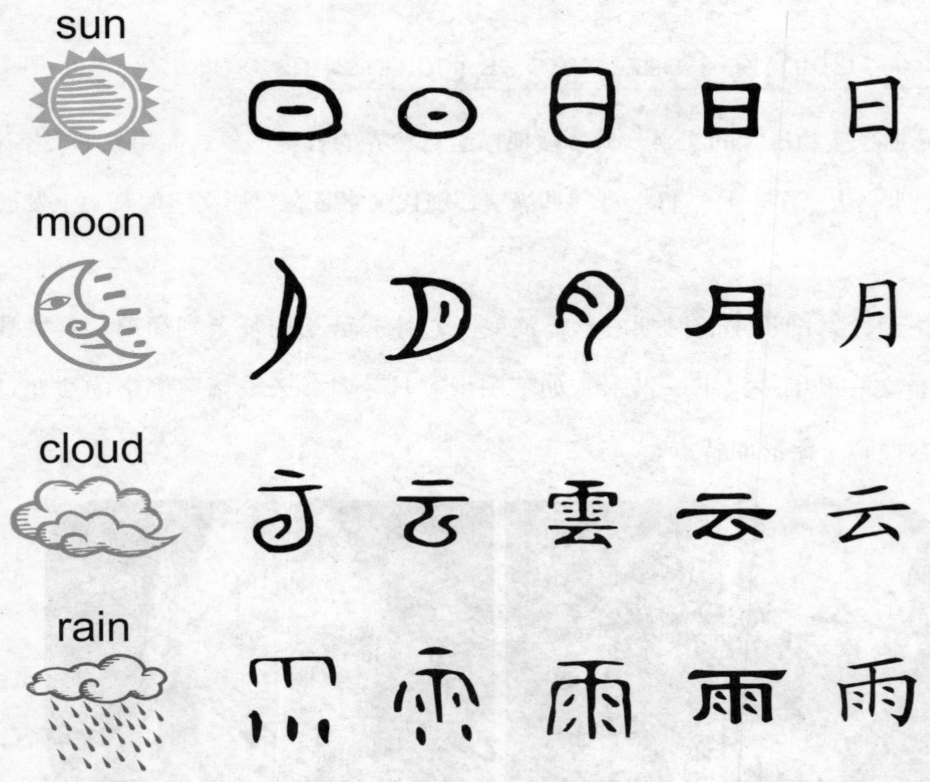

六、场景探索

场景一

1. 房子 fángzi house
2. 树 shù tree
3. 门 mén door
4. 草地 cǎodì grassy area
5. 路 lù road
6. 窗户 chuānghu window

场景二

1. 墙 qiáng wall
2. 窗户 chuānghu window
3. 天花板 tiānhuābǎn ceiling
4. 门 mén door
5. 地毯 dìtǎn carpet

第三集

他是谁

第三集　他是谁

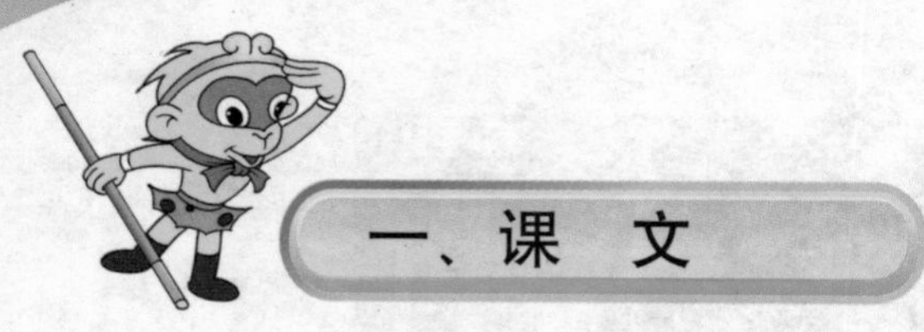

一、课　文

陆大伟：　马老师，他是谁？

马老师：　他是我弟弟。

陆大伟：　你弟弟真酷，他是警察吗？

马老师：　对，他是警察。

陆大伟：　马老师，她是谁？

马老师：　是我朋友，她也是老师。

罗　斯：　马老师好！

马老师：　罗斯，你好！这是陆大伟。大伟，这是罗斯。

陆大伟：　罗斯，你好！很高兴认识你！

罗　斯：　你好！啊，我知道你，脸谱！

陆大伟：　我也知道你，自行车！

Lù Dàwěi: Mǎ lǎoshī, tā shì shuí?
Mǎ Lǎoshī: Tā shì wǒ dìdi.
Lù Dàwěi: Nǐ dìdi zhēn kù, tā shì jǐngchá ma?
Mǎ Lǎoshī: Duì, tā shì jǐngchá.

Lù Dàwěi: Mǎ lǎoshī, tā shì shuí?
Mǎ Lǎoshī: Shì wǒ péngyou, tā yě shì lǎoshī.

Luósī: Mǎ lǎoshī hǎo!
Mǎ Lǎoshī: Luósī, nǐ hǎo! Zhè shì Lù Dàwěi. Dàwěi, zhè shì Luósī.
Lù Dàwěi: Luósī, nǐ hǎo! Hěn gāoxìng rènshi nǐ!
Luósī: Nǐ hǎo! À, wǒ zhīdào nǐ, liǎnpǔ!
Lù Dàwěi: Wǒ yě zhīdào nǐ, zìxíngchē!

David: Teacher Ma, who is he?
Teacher Ma: He's my younger brother.
David: Your younger brother's really cool. Is he a policeman?
Teacher Ma: Yes, he's a policeman.

David: Teacher Ma, who is she?
Teacher Ma: My friend. She is also a teacher.

Ross: Hello, Teacher Ma!
Teacher Ma: Ross, hello! This is Lu Dawei. Dawei, this is Ross.
David: Ross, hello! Pleased to meet you!
Ross: Hello! Ah, I know you, lianpu!
David: I know you too, bicycle!

⊙ 陆大伟：罗斯，这是孔子，对吗？

罗　斯：你知道孔子？

陆大伟：对，我知道，孔子是有名的老师！

罗　斯：对，孔子是有名的老师，我不是！

⊙ 陆大伟：罗斯，这是你的书吗？

罗　斯：这是马老师的书，这是我的书。

陆大伟：这是我们的书。

马老师：对，这是我们的书，《乘风汉语》！

⊙ 罗　斯：马老师，他是谁，是你弟弟吗？

马老师：对，是我弟弟，他是警察。这是我朋友，她也是老师。

罗　斯：大伟，你看，她的衣服真漂亮！

陆大伟：马老师，这是什么衣服？

马老师：这是旗袍！

⊙ Lù Dàwěi: Luósī, zhè shì Kǒngzǐ, duì ma?
Luósī: Nǐ zhīdào Kǒngzǐ?
Lù Dàwěi: Duì, wǒ zhīdào, Kǒngzǐ shì yǒumíng de lǎoshī!
Luósī: Duì, Kǒngzǐ shì yǒumíng de lǎoshī, wǒ bú shì!

⊙ Lù Dàwěi: Luósī, zhè shì nǐ de shū ma?
Luósī: Zhè shì Mǎ lǎoshī de shū, zhè shì wǒ de shū.
Lù Dàwěi: Zhè shì wǒmen de shū.
Mǎ Lǎoshī: Duì, zhè shì wǒmen de shū, Chéngfēng Hànyǔ!

⊙ Luósī: Mǎ lǎoshī, tā shì shuí, shì nǐ dìdi ma?
Mǎ Lǎoshī: Duì, shì wǒ dìdi, tā shì jǐngchá. Zhè shì wǒ péngyou, tā yě shì lǎoshī.
Luósī: Dàwěi, nǐ kàn, tā de yīfu zhēn piàoliang!
Lù Dàwěi: Mǎ lǎoshī, zhè shì shénme yīfu?
Mǎ Lǎoshī: Zhè shì qípáo!

⊙ David: Ross, this is Confucius, right?
Ross: You know Confucius?
David: Yes, I know. Confucius was a famous teacher!
Ross: Right, Confucius was a famous teacher, but I'm not!

⊙ David: Ross, is this your book?
Ross: This is Teacher Ma's book. This is my book.
David: This is our book!
Teacher Ma: Right, this is our book, Chengo Chinese!

⊙ Ross: Teacher Ma, who is he? Is he your younger brother?
Teacher Ma: Yes, (he's) my younger brother. He's a policeman. This is my friend. She is also a teacher.
Ross: David, look. Her clothing is really beautiful!
David: Teacher Ma, what (kind of) clothing is this?
Teacher Ma: This is a chi-pao!

二、词语表

1. 谁	shuí	who
2. 弟弟	dìdi	younger brother
3. 警察	jǐngchá	police; policeman
4. 她	tā	she; her
5. 朋友	péngyou	friend
6. 自行车	zìxíngchē	bike; bicycle
7. 孔子	Kǒngzǐ	Confucius
8. 有名	yǒumíng	famous
9. 的	de	particle (used after an attribute)
10. 我们	wǒmen	we; us
11. 书	shū	book
12. 乘风	Chéngfēng	Chengo
13. 汉语	Hànyǔ	Chinese
14. 看	kàn	look
15. 衣服	yīfu	clothing
16. 旗袍 *	qípáo	chi-pao

The symbol * indicates that the corresponding word is not practiced in this episode.

三、语言注释

我们的书

的 is often used to indicate possessive case or belonging just like -' s in English. Like "-' s", it should be placed in between the possessor and the possessee. e.g.

罗斯的自行车　　　　我们的老师　　　　中国的长城

马老师的书

马老师的弟弟

Please note: When the possessor is 我（们）、你（们）、他（们）, and the possessee is 朋友 or a term for a relative such as 姐姐、妈妈 etc., 的 is usually omitted. e.g.

我的弟弟 → 我弟弟　　　　你的姐姐 → 你姐姐　　　　他的朋友 → 他朋友

谁

谁 means who or whom, while 谁的 means whose. You can use 谁 to ask for information about a certain individual. Bear in mind that the usage of 谁 should follow the same word order as the following interrogative sentences:

谁是警察？

这是谁的书？

谁的弟弟是警察？

A：她是谁？

B：她是陆大伟的姐姐。

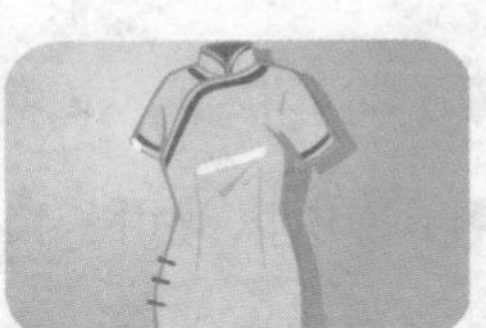

A：这是谁的旗袍？

B：这是王老师的旗袍。

四、汉　字

子 zǐ

古文字中，“子”的意思是“婴儿”，象婴儿在襁褓中，只留头、双臂在外，突出了婴儿脑袋比例大的特点。

“子”在古代指婴儿、孩子，今天则专指男孩。另外，古代“子”常用作对男子的尊称，如“孔子、孟子”。

In ancient Chinese script, 子 originally meant 婴儿（infant）. Its shape resembles an infant in swaddling clothes, with its head and two arms exposed, and which emphasizes the proportionally large head of an infant.

In ancient times, 子 signified infant or child, but nowadays it refers only to son or boy. Apart from this, 子, in ancient times, was often used as an honorific title for men, such as 孔子 (Confucius) or 孟子 (Mencius).

友 yǒu

古文字中，“友”是两只右手相加在一起，表示合作。因为朋友之间多进行合作，所以“友”的主要意思就是朋友，如“好友”。“友”也用来表示亲爱、友善，如“友邦”。

In ancient Chinese script, 友 represents two right hands joined together and signifies cooperation. And because friends will often cooperate with one another, the character 友 mainly means friend, such as 好友 (good friend). The character 友 can also mean “dear” or “friendly”, as in 友邦 (friendly nation).

自 zì

古文字中，“自”象人鼻子的形状，本义就是鼻子。人们在说到自己的时候，常喜欢用手指着自己的鼻子，所以就用“自”来表示“我”、“自己”。此后“自”的常用义就是第一人称代词，如“自尊、自信”等。

为了区别，就为“鼻子”这个意思又造了个“鼻”字。

In ancient Chinese 自 resembled the shape of a person's nose, and, in fact, originally meant just that. When talking about one's self, a person will often like to point toward his/her own nose. Thus, 自 came to be used to express 我 (I, me) or 自己 (oneself, self). Later on, the most commonly used meaning of 自 came to be as a first person pronoun, such as in 自尊 (self-respect), 自信 (self-confidence), etc.

In order to distinguish between these two different meanings, the character 鼻 was created to stand for nose（鼻子）.

行 xíng

古文字中，"行"象四通八达的路口之形，本义就是道路，读háng。这一意义在古文献里很常见。汉字中由"行"构成的字大多与道路有关，比如"街"。

道路是供人行走的，所以走路、行走也叫"行"，读xíng。这一意义是今天的常用义，如"行走、自行车"等。

The ancient form of the character 行 resembles the shape of an intersection leading out in all directions. It originally meant road, and, in this sense of the word, it is pronounced háng. This meaning of the character often appears in ancient Chinese texts. The meanings of most of the Chinese characters which are constructed from 行 have some relation to road, such as the character 街 (street).

Roads, of course, provide people a place to traverse or walk. Thus, walking or traveling on foot is also called 行. In this sense of the character, it is then pronounced xíng. It is this meaning of the word which is now the most common one. Some examples of this include 行走 (walk, go on foot) and 自行车 (bicycle).

朋

友

的

自

行

车

五、文化注释

中国的警察 Chinese Police

中国的警种设置分为九类，常见的有治安警察、刑事警察、交通警察、边防警察、消防警察、铁路警察等。

初中毕业生通过一定的考试，就可以进入警察学校，一般学习期限为三年。

▶ **相关信息**

中国现行的警服是1999年开始使用的。其颜色为藏青色或藏蓝色，与国际上警服通用的色调相一致。胸徽上明确标明警察所在的省份，右袖口还用汉语拼音标出“警察”两字。

China's police force has nine branches, the most common including public security police, criminal police, traffic police, border police, fire police, and railway police.

Policemen are generally recruited from graduates of police officer schools and public security universities. The former offers a three-year course for junior high school graduates whereas the latter, a four-year degree program for senior high school graduates. All the candidates should pass the entrance examinations at different levels before they are enrolled.

▶ **[Additional Notes]**

The police uniform currently worn throughout China was first adopted in 1999. It comes in either dark blue or navy blue, the same as police uniforms around the world. The symbol on the chest of the uniform clearly shows the province where the policeman works and “Jingcha”, the Chinese word for “Police” in Hanyu Pinyin (a Romanization system of Mandarin Chinese) is written on the right-hand cuff.

《论语》 The Confucian Analects

《论语》是记录孔子及其学生言论的一部儒家经典，据说是由孔子的弟子曾参的学生在战国初期最后编写成书的。《论语》对中国人的思想观念和行为规范有深刻的影响，其中不少言论至今仍然家喻户晓。比如“学而时习之”、“温故而知新”、“学而不厌，诲人不倦”、“有教无类”、“三思而后行”、“己所不欲，勿施于人”、“三人行，必有我师”、“四海之内皆兄弟也”、“有朋自远方来，不亦乐乎”等等。

The Confucian Analects, a classic work of Confucianism, is a collection of sayings by Confucius and his disciples. It is said that the compilation of the book was completed by the disciples of Zeng Shen, one of Confucius’ students, during the early years of the Warring States Period (475-221 B.C.). The Confucian Analects has had a strong influence on Chinese ideas and behavior. Many of the sayings in the book are well known among the Chinese people, these include: “learn and constantly carry into practice what has been learned”, “gain new knowledge by reviewing the old”, “learn painstakingly and tirelessly, teach with enthusiasm and patience”, “teach all without status distinctions”, “think thrice before you act”, “do not do to others what you would not have them do to you”, “Where three men walk together, one of them is bound to be able to teach me something”, “Within the four seas all men are brothers”, “Isn't it a delight to have friends coming from afar”, etc.

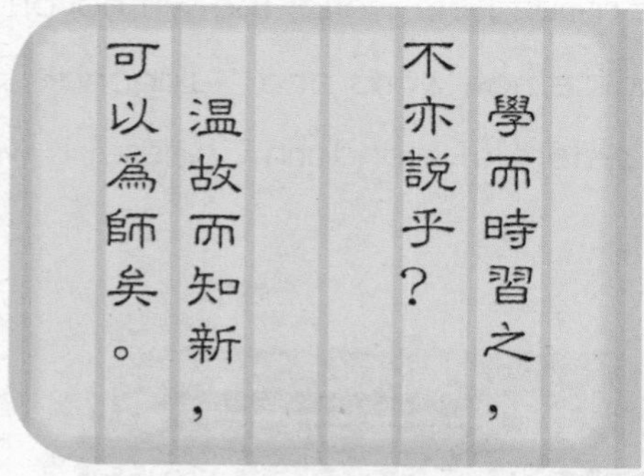

旗袍 Chi-pao

旗袍是中国的一种传统服装，线条简练优美，造型优雅大方，能充分展示女性的曲线美，深受妇女的喜爱。

▶ **相关信息**

旗袍原为中国满族妇女的民族服装。随着满汉生活的融合，旗袍被广大的汉族妇女所接受。目前，旗袍大多在正式场合上作为礼服来穿。

The Chi-pao is a traditional Chinese dress with simple but beautiful cut and elegant design that highlights the curves of the female body, and is therefore very popular among ladies.

▶ **[Additional Notes]**

The Chi-pao was originally the ethnic costume of China's Manchurian women. With the intermingling of Manchurian and Han peoples, the Chi-pao was adopted by the masses of Han women. Today, the Chi-pao is mostly used as a dress for formal occasions.

自行车　Bicycles

中国是世界上自行车生产量和拥有量最大的国家，素有“自行车王国”之称。自行车没有噪音和污染，是中国人的主要交通工具之一，许多人每天骑它上下班。在农村，有些人还将它当作运输工具。

▶ **相关信息**

近年来，中国人的交通方式日趋多元化，乘坐公共汽车、地铁和私人轿车的人不断增多。现在，自行车已经不再是中国人最重要的交通工具了，越来越多的人把它当成休闲和健身的器材。

Dubbed "a Bicycle Kingdom", China is the world's largest bicycle maker and user. Bicycles produce no noise or pollution and are a major mode of transport in China. Many people ride bicycles to and from work. In rural areas, some people even use them to transport goods.

[Additional Notes]

In recent years, modes of transport in China have become increasingly diverse. More and more people are using buses, the subway or private cars. Today, bicycles are no longer the primary mode of transport; but an increasing number of people are riding them for leisure and fitness purposes.

六、场景探索

场景一

1. 打印机 dǎyìnjī printer
2. 电脑 diànnǎo computer
3. 文件柜 wénjiànguì filing cabinet
4. 电话 diànhuà telephone
5. 台灯 táidēng desk lamp
6. 订书机 dìngshūjī stapler
7. 剪子 jiǎnzi scissors
8. 台历 táilì desk calendar
9. 胶带 jiāodài rubberized tape
10. 笔 bǐ pen

场景二

1. 杯子 bēizi cup
2. 茶叶桶 cháyètǒng tea caddy
3. 花盆 huāpén flowerpot
4. 植物 zhíwù plant
5. 相框 xiàngkuàng photo frame
6. 文件 wénjiàn file
7. 夹子 jiāzi document clasp
8. 词典 cídiǎn dictionary
9. 笔记本 bǐjìběn notebook

第四集

我有一个姐姐

第四集　我有一个姐姐

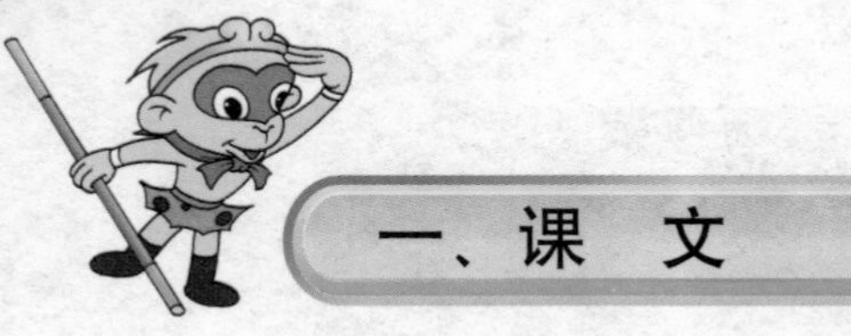

一、课　文

韩　江：大伟，这是什么字？你知道吗？

陆大伟：我知道，这是“山”。

韩　江：这个呢？

陆大伟：这个我不知道。啊，是“黄”字。

韩　江：“黄”，黄——山，黄山，我知道，我知道，黄山是中国有名的山。

陆大伟：对对对。你看，黄山！

韩　江：哎，她是谁？

陆大伟：是我姐姐。

韩　江：你姐姐喜欢旅行，是吗？

陆大伟：对，她喜欢旅行。我爸爸妈妈也喜欢旅行。你看，这是我爸爸、妈妈、姐姐、弟弟，这是我。

韩　江：一二三四五，你家有五口人。

陆大伟：对。你家呢，有几口人？

Hán Jiāng: Dàwěi, zhè shì shénme zì? Nǐ zhīdào ma?
Lù Dàwěi: Wǒ zhīdào, zhè shì "shān".
Hán Jiāng: Zhè ge ne?
Lù Dàwěi: Zhè ge wǒ bù zhīdào. À, shì "huáng" zì.
Hán Jiāng: "Huáng", huáng—shān, Huángshān, wǒ zhīdào, wǒ zhīdào, Huángshān shì Zhōngguó yǒumíng de shān.
Lù Dàwěi: Duì duì duì. Nǐ kàn, Huángshān!

Hán Jiāng: Éi, tā shì shuí?
Lù Dàwěi: Shì wǒ jiějie.
Hán Jiāng: Nǐ jiějie xǐhuan lǚxíng, shì ma?
Lù Dàwěi: Duì, tā xǐhuan lǚxíng. Wǒ bàba māma yě xǐhuan lǚxíng. Nǐ kàn, zhè shì wǒ bàba, māma, jiějie, dìdi, zhè shì wǒ.
Hán Jiāng: Yī èr sān sì wǔ, nǐ jiā yǒu wǔ kǒu rén.
Lù Dàwěi: Duì. Nǐ jiā ne, yǒu jǐ kǒu rén?

John: David, what character is this? Do you know?
David: I know. This is the character for "mountain".
John: And this?
David: I don't know what this is. Ah, it's the character for "yellow".
John: "Huang", Huang-Shan, Huang Shan, I know, I know. Huang Shan is a famous mountain in China.
David: Right! Right! Right! Look, Huang Shan!

John: Hey, who is she?
David: That's my elder sister.
John: Your elder sister likes traveling, doesn't she?
David: Yes, she likes traveling. My dad and mom like traveling, too. Look, these are my dad, mom, elder sister, and younger brother. This is me.
John: One, two, three, four, five. There are five people in your family.
David: Right. What about your family? How many people?

⊙ 韩　江：我家有四口人。爸爸、妈妈、姐姐、我。

陆大伟：还有呢？

韩　江：还有什么？

陆大伟：还有六口人呢？

韩　江：我家有四口人，不是十口人。

⊙ 韩　江：子欣，你知道吗？

王子欣：知道什么？

韩　江：大伟有一个姐姐。

王子欣：我知道，还有呢？

韩　江：他姐姐喜欢旅行！

王子欣：我知道，还有呢？

韩　江：还有……，还有黄山，你看！

王子欣：对，黄山，中国有名的山。还有呢？

韩　江：还有……，我不知道。大伟，还有什么？

陆大伟：我姐姐二十岁。

王子欣：我也知道，还有呢？

韩　江：我知道，我也知道，还有呢？子欣，你是警察吗？

Hán Jiāng: Wǒ jiā yǒu sì kǒu rén. Bàba, māma, jiějie, wǒ.
Lù Dàwěi: Hái yǒu ne?
Hán Jiāng: Hái yǒu shénme?
Lù Dàwěi: Hái yǒu liù kǒu rén ne?
Hán Jiāng: Wǒ jiā yǒu sì kǒu rén, bú shì shí kǒu rén.

Hán Jiāng: Zǐxīn, nǐ zhīdào ma?
Wáng Zǐxīn: Zhīdào shénme?
Hán Jiāng: Dàwěi yǒu yí gè jiějie.
Wáng Zǐxīn: Wǒ zhīdào, hái yǒu ne?
Hán Jiāng: Tā jiějie xǐhuan lǚxíng!
Wáng Zǐxīn: Wǒ zhīdào, hái yǒu ne?
Hán Jiāng: Hái yǒu…… hái yǒu Huángshān, nǐ kàn!
Wáng Zǐxīn: Duì, Huángshān, Zhōngguó yǒumíng de shān. Hái yǒu ne?
Hán Jiāng: Hái yǒu……wǒ bù zhīdào. Dàwěi, hái yǒu shénme?
Lù Dàwěi: Wǒ jiějie èrshí suì.
Wáng Zǐxīn: Wǒ yě zhīdào, hái yǒu ne?
Hán Jiāng: Wǒ zhīdào, wǒ yě zhīdào, hái yǒu ne? Zǐxīn, nǐ shì jǐngchá ma?

John: There are four people in my family. Dad, Mom, Elder sister and me.
David: Anybody else?
John: What else?
David: What about the six other people?
John: There are four people in my family, not ten people.

John: Cindy, did you know?
Cindy: Know what?
John: David has an elder sister.
Cindy: I know. What else?
John: His elder sister likes traveling.
Cindy: I know. What else?
John: And…, and Huang Shan. Look!
Cindy: Yes, Huang Shan, a famous Chinese mountain. What else?
John: And…, I don' t know. David, what else?
David: My elder sister is 20 years old.
Cindy: I also know. What else?
John: I know, I also know, and what else? Cindy, are you a policewoman?

二、词语表

1. 黄山	Huángshān	Huang Shan; Huangshan Mountain; Yellow Mountain
2. 个	gè	a measure word
3. 中国	Zhōngguó	China
4. 姐姐	jiějie	elder sister
5. 喜欢	xǐhuan	to like; to love; to be fond of
6. 旅行	lǚxíng	to travel
7. 爸爸	bàba	father; dad
8. 妈妈	māma	mother; mom
9. 一	yī	one
10. 二	èr	two
11. 三	sān	three
12. 四	sì	four
13. 五	wǔ	five
14. 家	jiā	family
15. 几	jǐ	how many; several
16. 口	kǒu	a measure word
17. 人	rén	people
18. 呢	ne	particle (used at the end of a question)
19. 还	hái	still; also
20. 有	yǒu	to have
21. 二十	èrshí	twenty
22. 岁	suì	a measure word for age
23. 哎 *	éi	interjection (showing surprise or disapproval)
24. 六 *	liù	six
25. 十 *	shí	ten

The symbol * indicates that the corresponding word is not practiced in this episode.

三、语言注释

个&口

口&个 function like "cup" or "piece" in English phrases such as "a cup of water, a piece of news". These kinds of words are placed in between numbers and nouns, and are frequently called "measure words" or "classifiers". Almost every noun in Chinese has a specific measure word. The most common one is 个, as in the following:

一个老师　三个姐姐　五个脸谱　六个人

一个警察

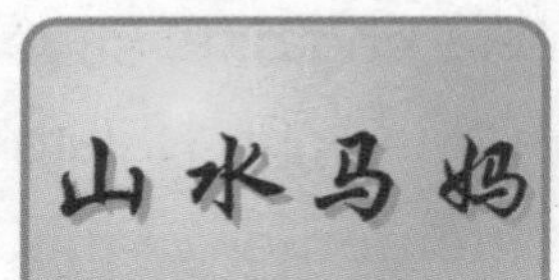

四个字

口 is mostly used as a measure word for family members. For example:

三口人　五口人

几

If you want to ask how much or how many, you can use 几. Keep in mind that you should always add a measure word after 几. e.g.

你有几个老师?

你家有几口人?

A：大伟家有几口人?

B：他家有五口人。

A：王子欣有几个熊猫?

B：她有一个熊猫。

四、汉 字

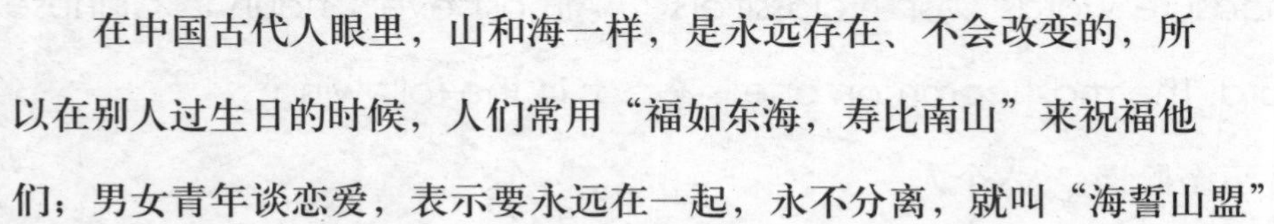

山 shān

古文字中，“山”象山峦起伏、山峰并立之形，本义就是山。“山”多用于山名，如“黄山、泰山”。

在中国古代人眼里，山和海一样，是永远存在、不会改变的，所以在别人过生日的时候，人们常用“福如东海，寿比南山”来祝福他们；男女青年谈恋爱，表示要永远在一起，永不分离，就叫“海誓山盟”。

The ancient form of the Chinese character 山 resembles the shape of a chain of mountain peaks, side-by-side, and uneven in height. Naturally, its original meaning is mountain. The character 山 is mainly used in the names of mountains, such as 黄山 (Yellow Mountain) and 泰山 (Tai Mountain). In the eyes of the ancient Chinese, mountains and oceans alike were considered to be eternal and unchanging. Thus, when someone has a birthday, Chinese people like to express their best wishes to that person by saying, 福如东海，寿比南山 (May your happiness be as boundless as the Eastern Sea and may you live as long as the South Mountain.). When two young lovers vow to stay with each other forever and never part, Chinese will often describe this as 海誓山盟 (A pledge between the mountain and the sea), which conveys the idea of a solemn vow of eternal love.

家 jiā

“家”本义是人的住所。古文字中，“家”上面是房子的形状，下面是一头猪。从字形来看，“家”居然是养猪的地方，是猪圈。那么，猪圈和人的住所有什么关系呢？

在远古的时候，人类靠采摘果实、捕鱼打猎为生，后来慢慢学会了驯养野兽。猪在很早时就被人类驯化了，当时条件简陋，人和猪是住在同一个屋子里的。后来，随着生活水平的提高，人不再跟猪住在同一个屋子里，“家”变成了专门供人居住的场所。

另外，“家”还指掌握某种专门学识或者从事某种专门活动的人，如“画家、科学家、历史学家”。

The original meaning of 家 is residence or human dwelling. In ancient Chinese script, the top half of the character 家 is the shape of a house while the bottom half represents a pig. From the shape of the character, 家 is actually a place for raising pigs, a pigsty! So, you may ask, what is the connection between a pigsty and a human dwelling?

Well, in remote antiquity, mankind once relied on gathering fruits and hunting animals such as fish and pigs. Over time, man learned to domesticate wild animals. Humans domesticated pigs quite early on. However, conditions were very primitive and crude at that time, and so humans and pigs lived together under the same roof. Later on, as living conditions improved, people no longer lived together with pigs. Thus, the character 家 changed to mean a residence only used for humans.

Apart from meaning home, 家 is also used to indicate a person who has mastered some type of knowledge or skill. Examples of this meaning include: 画家 (painter), 科学家 (scientist), and 历史学家 (historian).

口 kǒu

古文字中，“口”象人嘴的形状，本义就是人、动物的嘴，如“口语”。也指出入的通道，如“门口、入口、洞口”。

民以食为天，古人生活条件不好，首先要解决的就是吃饭问题，“口”就成了人的最重要的特征，因而也可用于指人，如“人口、拖家带口”；又可以用作人的量词，如“我家有三口人”。

In ancient script 口 resembles a human mouth and its earliest meaning was the mouth of a person or animal, as can be seen from the word 口语 (spoken language). This character can also denote a passageway for exiting or entering, as in the following: 门口 (doorway; entrance; gate), 入口 (entrance; entry), or 洞口 (mouth or entrance of a cave) . As the Chinese saying goes, “For people, food is everything” . This expression reflects the fact that living conditions were quite harsh in ancient times, and the key aspect of daily life at that time which was just finding enough food to survive. Thus 口 came to represent the most important characteristic of human beings, and so, in Chinese, mouth also means person. Examples of this sense of the character include: 人口 (population) and 拖家带口 (be tied down by one’s family). This character can also be used as a measure word for people, as in 我家有三口人 (There are three people in my family.).

人 rén

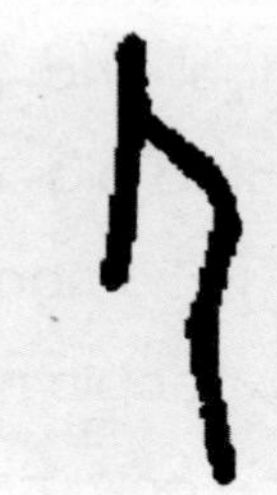

古文字中，“人”象一个人侧面站立的形状，可见其头、身体和一只手臂。本义就是人，如“男人、女人、人类”。也可以指某种人，如“客人、工人、北京人”。

“人”是汉字最常用的偏旁之一。由“人”构成的汉字，其意义大多与人或人的行为有关。人作偏旁时，在左边都写作“亻”，在其他部位仍然写作“人”。

In ancient Chinese, the character 人 looks like the side view of a standing person with a visible head, body and arm, and it originally means human or person. Some examples of this include: 男人 (man), 女人 (woman), and 人类 (mankind). It can also be used to indicate a particular kind of person. For example, 客人 (guest), 工人 (worker), and 北京人 (Beijinger). 人 is also one of the most commonly used radicals (basic component) in Chinese characters. The meanings of most of the Chinese Characters formed using 人 are related to people or human behavior. When the character 人 is used as a radical to be placed on the left-hand side of a character it is written as 亻, but, when used in any other position, it is still written as 人 .

中 zhōng

古文字中，“中”象旗子插在空地的中央之形。古代每遇大事发生，先把旗子插上，群众望见了便从四面八方汇聚到旗子下。“中”字的本义就是中央、中间。

中国古代人认为天圆地方，而中国在地的中央，所以称“中国”，简称“中”，如“中外、中美”。

In ancient script, 中 resembles the shape of a flag planted in the center of an open ground. Whenever an important event took place in ancient times, a flag was first erected. Upon seeing it, the masses would then come from all directions to gather under it. The original meaning of 中 is center or middle.

The ancient Chinese believed that the heavens were round and that earth was square. They also saw China as being in the center of the earth and thus referred to it as 中国 (the Central Nation or "Middle Kingdom"). In Chinese, the abbreviated form of 中国 is 中 as in 中外 (Sino-foreign; In China and abroad) and 中美 (Sino-U.S.; Sino-American).

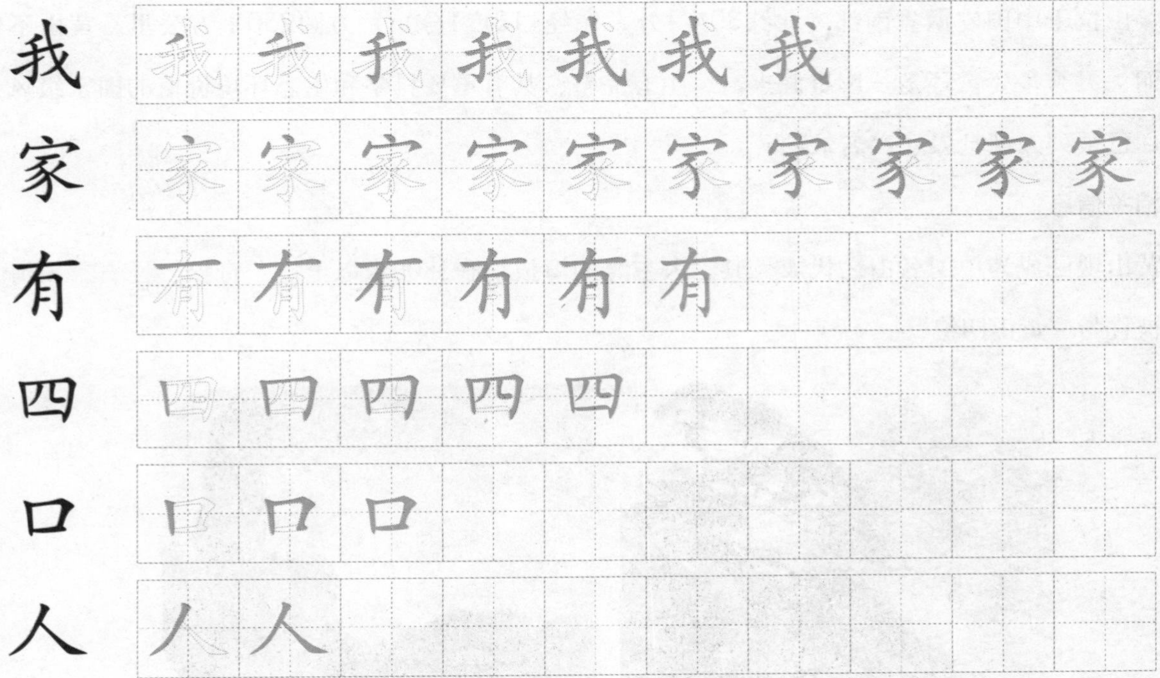

五、文化注释

黄山 Mt. Huangshan

黄山位于中国安徽省南部（北纬30度1分，东经118度1分），方圆250平方公里。黄山不仅奇伟俏丽、灵秀多姿，还是一座资源丰富、生态完整、具有重要科学和生态环境价值的国家级风景名胜区，已被列入《世界遗产名录》。

▶ 相关信息

黄山现已成为中国名山之代表，其三大主峰的海拔均在1800米以上。“奇松、怪石、云海、温泉”被称为“黄山四绝”。

Mt. Huangshan (Latitude 30.1° N., Longitude 118.1° E.) is located in southern Anhui Province and covers an area of about 250 square kilometers. Well known for its magnificent scenery, Huang Shan is a major national tourist site. With its rich resources and well-preserved ecological diversity, it is also an area of great scientific and ecological significance. Huang Shan was included in UNESCO's list of World Heritage Sites in 1990.

▶ [Additional Notes]

Huang Shan is perhaps the best example of mountain scenery in China. The average altitude of its three main peaks reaches over 1,800 meters. Moreover, it boasts oddly shaped pines, unique rock formations, sea of clouds and crystal-clear mountain springs which are collectively known as its “four superb scenes”.

中国的家庭 Families in China

目前，中国家庭的特点是日趋小型化，单亲家庭、无子女家庭和只有一个子女的家庭已占一定比例，但中国仍然是“亲情社会”，亲戚之间依然来往频繁；需要帮助时，“家人”仍是大多数人选择的对象。

▶ 相关信息

传统的中国家庭往往是三代同堂（父母、孩子、祖父母），有的甚至是四代同堂。这是因为中国人比较重视亲情关系，喜欢与家人或亲属生活在一起。

随着现代经济的发展，特别是计划生育政策的实施，传统的家庭结构正在发生变化，现代家庭变得越来越小，亲属关系也越来越简单。由一对夫妇和他们的未婚独生子女组成的核心家庭正在成为中国社会（特别是城市）主要的家庭模式。这种家庭对亲属关系网的依赖程度较低，子女不一定与父母和其他长辈共同居住。

In present-day China, families are becoming smaller in size. Single-parent families, DINK families, and single-child families now make up a certain percentage of the Chinese population. However, China remains a society that places a high value on close family ties. Therefore, frequent visits among relatives are quite common and Chinese almost always look to family members for help in times of difficulty.

▶ [Additional Notes]

The traditional Chinese family is usually an extended family, with three generations (parents, children and grandparents), or sometimes even four generations, living under the same roof. Chinese generally have a strong sense of family and like to live with their family members or relatives.

With the development of a modern economy, and especially after the enforcement of the one-child policy, there have been considerable changes in the traditional family structure. Modern families are getting smaller and familial relationships have become simpler. The nuclear family, composed of parents and an unmarried child, has become a major family structure in China, especially in cities. As this kind of family pattern has a lower dependency on kinship ties, children do not necessarily live with their parents or other elder members of the family.

 手势与数字 Chinese Hand Gestures for Numbers

中国人用手势表示数字，如图所示。

Chinese people use their own unique hand gestures to indicate the numbers from 1 to 10 as illustrated in the pictures below:

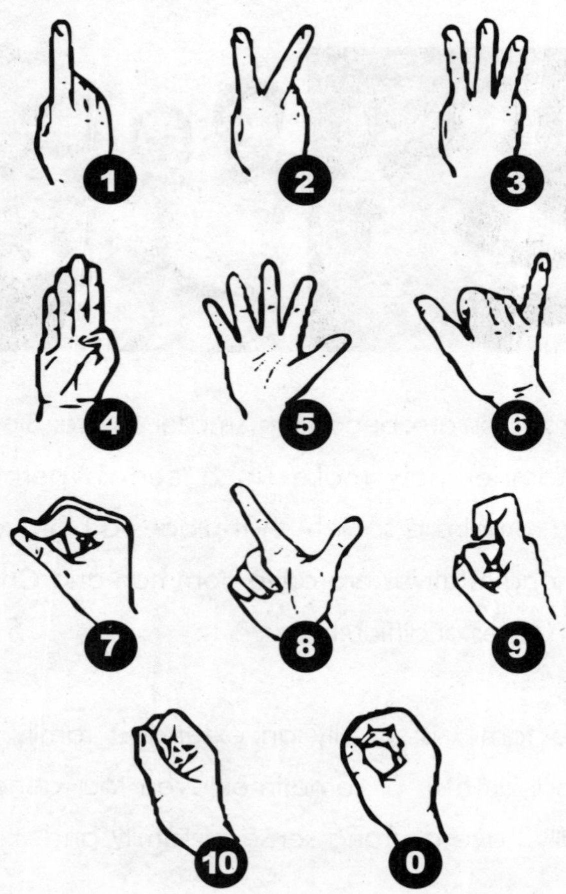

六、场景探索

场景一

1. 橄榄球	gǎnlǎnqiú	rugby
2. 桌子	zhuōzi	desk
3. 垃圾桶	lājītǒng	trash can
4. 窗帘	chuānglián	curtain
5. 画	huà	painting
6. 台灯	táidēng	desk lamp
7. 电脑	diànnǎo	computer
8. 椅子	yǐzi	chair
9. 地毯	dìtǎn	carpet
10. 墙	qiáng	wall
11. 花	huā	flower
12. 书	shū	book

场景二

1. 桌子	zhuōzi	desk
2. 地毯	dìtǎn	carpet
3. 门	mén	door
4. 沙发	shāfā	sofa
5. 靠垫	kàodiàn	back cushion
6. 台灯	táidēng	desk lamp
7. 墙	qiáng	wall
8. 画	huà	painting

第五集

房间里有松鼠

第五集　房间里有松鼠

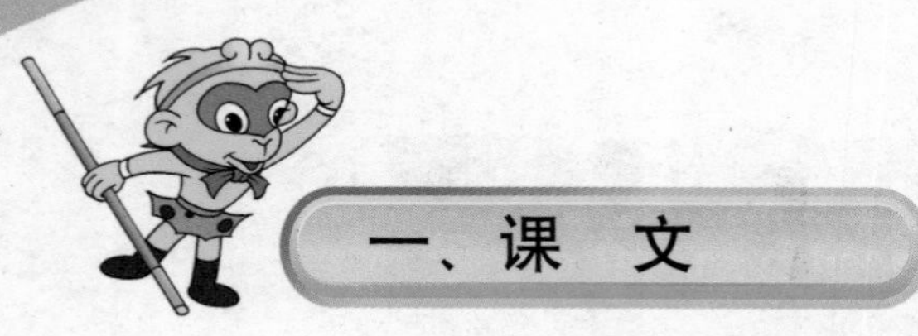

一、课 文

王子欣： 这里有山有水，真漂亮！

陆大伟： 我也喜欢山，但是不喜欢水。

韩 江： 大伟、子欣！ 我有一个很酷的东西。

王子欣： 什么东西？

韩 江： 看！

陆大伟： 这是什么？

王子欣： 我知道，我知道！这是二……二胡！

陆大伟： 二胡？

韩 江： 对，一二三四的“二”。

陆大伟： 哈哈！

⊙ Wáng Zǐxīn: Zhèlǐ yǒu shān yǒu shuǐ, zhēn piàoliang!

Lù Dàwěi: Wǒ yě xǐhuan shān, dànshì bù xǐhuan shuǐ.

⊙ Hán Jiāng: Dàwěi、Zǐxīn! Wǒ yǒu yí gè hěn kù de dōngxi.

Wáng Zǐxīn: Shénme dōngxi?

Hán Jiāng: Kàn!

Lù Dàwěi: Zhè shì shénme?

Wáng Zǐxīn: Wǒ zhīdào, wǒ zhīdào! Zhè shì èr …… èrhú!

Lù Dàwěi: Èrhú?

Hán Jiāng: Duì, yī èr sān sì de “èr” .

Lù Dàwěi: Hāhā!

⊙ Cindy: There are mountains and water here. It’s really beautiful!

David: I like mountains too, but I don’t like water.

⊙ John: David, Cindy! I have something pretty cool to show you.

Cindy: What is it?

John: Look!

David: What’s this?

Cindy: I know, I know! This is an er...erhu.

David: Erhu?

John: Right, “2” in 1-2-3-4.

David: Ha ha!

王子欣：韩江，你喜欢音乐吗？

韩　江：对，我喜欢中国音乐，我喜欢二胡。你呢，你喜欢什么？

王子欣：我喜欢流行音乐，我也喜欢这个。

一二三四五，

上山采蘑菇。

蘑菇没采到，

碰到小松鼠。

松鼠有几个？

一二三四五。

韩　江：一二三四五，我有小松鼠。

陆大伟：松鼠很可爱，我也喜欢松鼠。

⊙ Wáng Zǐxīn: Hán Jiāng, nǐ xǐhuan yīnyuè ma?

Hán Jiāng: Duì, wǒ xǐhuan Zhōngguó yīnyuè, wǒ xǐhuan èrhú. Nǐ ne, nǐ xǐhuan shénme?

Wáng Zǐxīn: Wǒ xǐhuan liúxíng yīnyuè, wǒ yě xǐhuan zhège.
Yī èr sān sì wǔ,
Shàng shān cǎi mógu.
Mógu méi cǎi dào,
Pèng dào xiǎo sōngshǔ.
Sōngshǔ yǒu jǐ gè?
Yī èr sān sì wǔ.

Hán Jiāng: Yī èr sān sì wǔ, wǒ yǒu xiǎo sōngshǔ.

Lù Dàwěi: Sōngshǔ hěn kě' ài, wǒ yě xǐhuan sōngshǔ.

⊙ Cindy: John, do you like music?

John: Yes, I like Chinese music and I like erhu. And you? What do you like?

Cindy: I like pop music, and I like this, too.
One-two-three-four-five,
we climbed the mountain to pick mushrooms.
We didn' t pick any,
but we met some little squirrels on the way.
How many squirrels were there?
One-two-three-four-five.

John: One-two-three-four-five, I have little squirrels.

David: Squirrels are so cute. I like squirrels, too.

韩　江：子欣，你的房间里有小松鼠吗？

王子欣：我的房间里有桌子、椅子，有电脑、电话，但是，没有小松鼠。

韩　江：没有？你看，那是什么？

陆大伟：啊……！

王子欣：小松鼠！我的房间里有小松鼠！

陆大伟：啊……！你的房间里还有蘑菇！

王子欣：这是台灯，不是蘑菇！

Hán Jiāng: Zǐxīn, nǐ de fángjiān li yǒu xiǎo sōngshǔ ma?

Wáng Zǐxīn: Wǒ de fángjiān li yǒu zhuōzi, yǐzi, yǒu diànnǎo, diànhuà, dànshì, méiyǒu xiǎo sōngshǔ.

Hán Jiāng: Méiyǒu? Nǐ kàn, nà shì shénme?

Lù Dàwěi: Á…… !

Wáng Zǐxīn: Xiǎo sōngshǔ! Wǒ de fángjiān li yǒu xiǎo sōngshǔ!

Lù Dàwěi: Á…… ! Nǐ de fángjiān li hái yǒu mógu!

Wáng Zǐxīn: Zhè shì táidēng, bú shì mógu!

John: Cindy, are there some little squirrels in your room?

Cindy: In my room I have a desk, a chair, a computer, and a telephone in my room, but not any little squirrels.

John: No? Look! What's that?

David: Ah...!

Cindy: Little squirrels! There are little squirrels in my room!

David: Ah...! There is also a mushroom in your room.

Cindy: This is a desk lamp, not a mushroom!

二、词语表

1. 这里	zhèlǐ	here
2. 水	shuǐ	river; water
3. 但是	dànshì	but; however
4. 东西	dōngxi	thing(s)
5. 二胡	èrhú	erhu, a two-stringed bowed instrument
6. 音乐	yīnyuè	music
7. 流行	liúxíng	popular
8. 小	xiǎo	small; little
9. 松鼠	sōngshǔ	squirrel
10. 房间	fángjiān	room
11. 里	lǐ	inside
12. 桌子	zhuōzi	table; desk
13. 椅子	yǐzi	chair
14. 电脑	diànnǎo	computer
15. 电话	diànhuà	telephone
16. 没有	méiyǒu	there is not; not have
17. 那	nà	that
18. 蘑菇	mógu	mushroom
19. 台灯	táidēng	desk lamp

三、语言注释

有/没有

有 can be used to express possession or existence similar to have/has or there is/are in English. Its negative form is 没有. e.g.

陆大伟有一个姐姐。

韩江有二胡，陆大伟没有。

房间里有小松鼠，没有蘑菇。

A：韩江的房间里有橄榄球吗？

B：有，他的房间里有橄榄球。

A：王子欣的房间里有电脑吗？

B：有，她的房间里有电脑。

可爱 (adjectives)

If we want to describe a person, object or a place, we can use adjectives such as 可爱, 漂亮, 有名, 好, 酷 etc. In Chinese adjectives are often used together with adverbs such as 很, 真 etc. to emphasize them. But Chinese adjectives are not usually used directly with 是 as common in English with " is" ! Generally, you should avoid using 是 directly in front of adjectives in Chinese. e.g.

熊猫很可爱。

马老师很漂亮。

王子欣的房间真好!

姚明真酷!

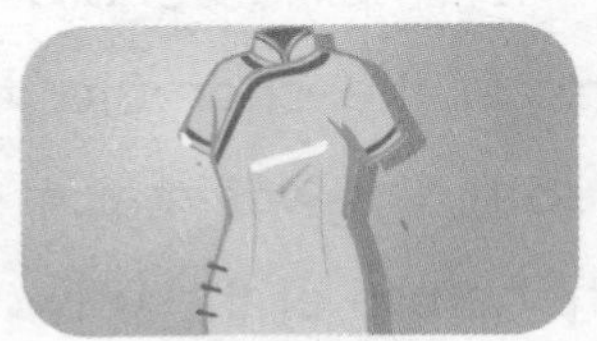

旗袍很漂亮。

四、汉　字

水 shuǐ

古文字中，“水”中间象水流之形，两边的小点儿象水滴。“水”的本义是河流。中国古代有一本专门讲河流的地理书，就叫《水经》。

“水”在今天的常用意义是指饮用、洗涤之水，如“矿泉水、自来水”；也可以指像水一样的东西，如“墨水、药水”。

The middle section of the ancient form of the character 水 resembles the shape of flowing water while the small dots on either end resemble water drops. The original meaning of 水 is river. In fact, one Chinese geographical text written in ancient times concerning rivers is entitled 水经 (The Waterways Classic).

Nowadays, the most common meaning for 水 is to refer to water used for drinking or washing. For example, 矿泉水（mineral water）or 自来水（tap water）. This character can also be used to describe things like water such as 墨水（ink）or 药水（liquid medicine）.

乐 yuè

“乐”繁体字是“樂”。古文字中，“乐”上面是丝，下面是木头，象用丝和木头制作成的乐器之形。在古代文献里，“乐”既可以用指乐器，也可以指音乐。“乐”的“音乐”义是今天的常用意义，如“乐队”。用于以上意义时，“乐”都读yuè。

此外，“乐”还读lè，意思是愉快、高兴，如“快乐、欢乐”。

The classical form of the simplified character 乐 is written as 樂. From the latter, we can see that the ancient form of the character contains the radical for string on top and the radical for wood underneath. This was meant to resemble the shape of a musical instrument which was made through the use of these two materials. Within ancient texts, 乐 was used to indicate musical instrument or music. In present-day Chinese, it is most commonly used to refer to music. When used to indicate the above two meanings, this character is pronounced yuè.

In addition, 乐 can also be pronounced lè. When this pronunciation for the character is used, its meaning becomes happy or joyful. Two examples of this include 快乐 (cheerful; pleased) and 欢乐 (joyous; cheery; fun-filled).

东 dōng

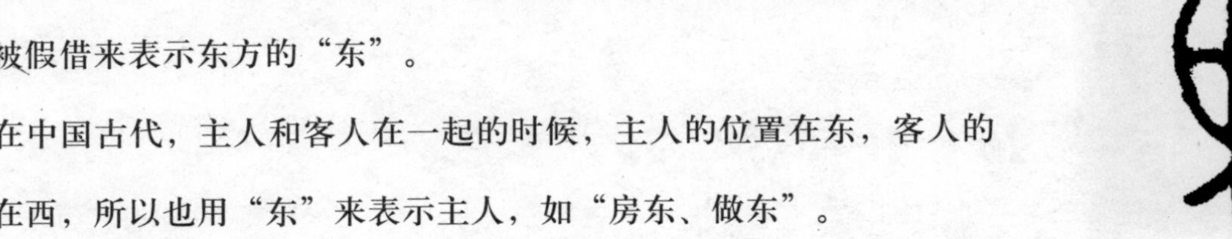

“东”繁体字是“東”。古文字中，“东”象里面装着东西、两头被扎起来的大口袋之形。但这个字在实际使用中并不是大口袋的意思，而是被假借来表示东方的“东”。

在中国古代，主人和客人在一起的时候，主人的位置在东，客人的位置在西，所以也用“东”来表示主人，如“房东、做东”。

The classical form of the character 东 is written as 東. In ancient script, 东 resembles the shape of a large sack filled with something and tied together at both ends. However, this character does not convey the meaning of a large sack in actual use, but rather is a phonetic loan character used to express “east (东)” as of eastern or oriental.

In ancient China, when a host and a guest sat together, the position of the host was always east while that of the guest was always west. Thus, 东 is also used to express the meaning of host. Examples of this include, 房东 (landlord) and 做东 (act as host).

他	他	他	他	他	他					
喜	喜	喜	喜	喜	喜	喜	喜	喜	喜	喜
	喜	喜								
欢	欢	欢	欢	欢	欢	欢				
音	音	音	音	音	音	音	音	音	音	
乐	乐	乐	乐	乐	乐					

二胡 Erhu

二胡音色优美、表现力强，是中国主要的乐器之一。用二胡演奏的著名曲目有《二泉映月》、《梁祝》、《江河水》等。著名演奏家有20世纪20年代的华彦钧（阿炳）和刘天华等。

As one of the most important musical instruments in China, the Erhu is a two-stringed bowed fiddle. When played, it produces beautiful tones and is very expressive of feelings. There are many famous Erhu pieces, like the well-known "The Moon Reflected on the Second Spring", "Liang Zhu", "The Water of Rivers", etc. Famous Erhu players include Hua Yanjun (Known as Ah Bing) and Liu Tianhua who became popular in the 1920's.

中国民乐 Traditional Chinese Music

中国的民乐种类繁多，各具特色。按照演奏习惯和乐器性能可以分为吹、拉、弹、打四大类器乐。中国乐曲大都和舞蹈结合在一起，在戏曲和曲艺形式中得到发展，有许多优秀的唱腔和舞台音乐。此外，还有不少带有地方色彩的民歌，如号子、山歌和小调，音调生动形象，具有浓厚的生活气息。

相关信息

吹管乐器有笛、箫、管、唢呐等。拉弦乐器有各种胡琴及少数民族乐器马头琴等。弹弦和打弦乐器有琵琶、三弦、古琴、筝、扬琴等。打击乐器有鼓类、锣类、钹类、板梆类等。这些乐器除了独奏外，还有各种合奏形式：有打击乐合奏、管乐合奏、弦乐合奏等等。

There are various kinds of folk music for traditional instruments in China, each one with its own unique features. These are categorized into four groups according to the way they are played: blown, pulled, plucked and beaten. Traditional Chinese music pieces are usually combined with dances. With the development of traditional Chinese theater and other forms of folk performing art, many good arias and stage pieces emerged. Also common in China are other forms of folk music such as working chants, folk songs and ditties. They have lively melodies and rich local flavor.

[Additional Notes]

Wind instruments: flute, vertical bamboo flute, tubular pipe and suona horn, etc. String instruments: many kinds of huqin (two-stringed) and matouqin (a bowed stringed instrument with a scroll carved in the image of a horse' s head mainly used by the Mongolians). Plucked instruments: pipa (four-stringed), sanxian (three-stringed), guzheng (long stringed instrument made of wood) and dulcimer, etc. Percussion instruments: drums, gongs, cymbals, wooden clappers, etc. These instruments can be played solo or in ensembles: instrumental percussion ensemble, wind ensemble, string ensemble, etc.

家居物品 Common Household Furniture and Necessities

中国家庭除了有家具（如床、衣橱、桌子、椅子、沙发、茶几）、家用电器（如电视机、录像机、VCD或DVD影碟机、电冰箱、空调、电热水器）、办公用品（如电话、传真机、电脑）等外，还有一些反映中国文化或者体现主人喜好的物品。比如，客厅或书房的墙壁上一般会悬挂中国画和书法作品，或者摆设一些中国瓷器和传统工艺美术品。有些中国人还喜欢在客厅摆鱼缸，在阳台上放置盆栽和盆景，或者笼养一些鸟类。

Apart from the necessary furniture (bed, closet, tables, chairs, sofa, tea table), electrical equipment (TV, video recorder, VCD or DVD player, refrigerator, air-conditioner, electric water heater) and office equipment (telephone, fax, computer), there are some other things commonly found in Chinese homes which clearly reflect Chinese culture and the taste of the owner. For example, Chinese paintings and works of calligraphy are often hung on the walls of the living room or study and Chinese porcelain and traditional handicrafts are placed around the rooms. Some Chinese people also like to place a fish tank in the lounge, put bonsai trees or artificial rockeries on the balcony, or keep some birds in a cage.

六、场景探索

场景一

1. 草地 cǎodì grassy area
2. 水 shuǐ water
3. 山 shān mountain
4. 云 yún cloud
5. 树 shù tree
6. 鸟 niǎo bird

场景二

1. 画 huà painting
2. 闹钟 nàozhōng alarm clock
3. 音箱 yīnxiāng speakers
4. 鼠标 shǔbiāo (computer) mouse
5. 可乐 kělè coke
6. 玩具 wánjù toy
7. 键盘 jiànpán keyboard
8. 书 shū book
9. 相框 xiàngkuàng photo frame

第六集

在美国北边

第六集　在美国北边

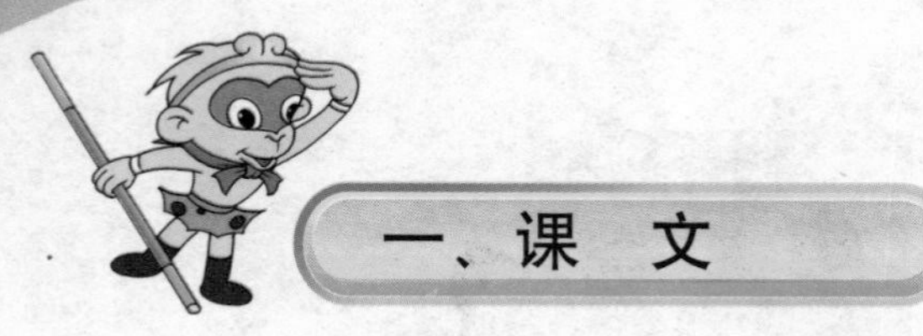

一、课　文

⊙ 陆大伟：你好，张老师！

张校长：你好，大伟！有课吗？

陆大伟：我有地理课，但是不知道教室在哪儿。

张校长：哦，在二楼，第一个教室。

陆大伟：谢谢张老师！

张校长：不客气。

⊙ 马老师：这是什么，你们知道吗？

王子欣：这是中国地图！

马老师：对。你们看，长城在哪儿？

陆大伟：长城在北边。

马老师：对，长城在中国北边。

Lù Dàwěi:	Nǐ hǎo, Zhāng lǎoshī!
Zhāng Xiàozhǎng:	Nǐ hǎo, Dàwěi! Yǒu kè ma?
Lù Dàwěi:	Wǒ yǒu dìlǐ kè, dànshì bù zhīdào jiàoshì zài nǎr.
Zhāng Xiàozhǎng:	Zài èr lóu, dì yī gè jiàoshì.
Lù Dàwěi:	Xièxie Zhāng lǎoshī!
Zhāng Xiàozhǎng:	Búkèqi.

Mǎ Lǎoshī:	Zhè shì shénme, nǐmen zhīdào ma?
Wáng Zǐxīn:	Zhè shì Zhōngguó dìtú!
Mǎ Lǎoshī:	Duì. Nǐmen kàn, Chángchéng zài nǎr?
Lù Dàwěi:	Chángchéng zài běibiān.
Mǎ Lǎoshī:	Duì, Chángchéng zài Zhōngguó běi biān.

David:	Hello, Teacher Zhang!
Principal Zhang:	Hello, David! Do you have class?
David:	I have geography class, but I don't know where the classroom is.
Principal Zhang:	Oh, it's the first classroom on the second floor.
David:	Thank you, Teacher Zhang.
Principal Zhang:	Don't mention it.

Teacher Ma:	What's this? Do you know?
Cindy:	This is a Chinese map.
Teacher Ma:	Right. Everyone takes a look. Where is the Great Wall?
David:	The Great Wall is in the north.
Teacher Ma:	Right, the Great Wall is in the northern part of China.

⊙ 王子欣：黄山呢，黄山在哪儿？

韩　江：这个我知道！黄山在这儿。

⊙ 马老师：美国在哪儿？

陆大伟：美国在这儿！

马老师：对，这是美国，这是中国。

韩　江：中间是什么？

王子欣：是太平洋，你们看，我家在太平洋上！在这儿，夏威夷！

马老师：对，夏威夷在太平洋上。

⊙	Wáng Zǐxīn:	Huángshān ne, Huángshān zài nǎr?
	Hán Jiāng:	Zhège wǒ zhīdào! Huángshān zài zhèr.

⊙	Mǎ Lǎoshī:	Měiguó zài nǎr?
	Lù Dàwěi:	Měiguó zài zhèr!
	Mǎ Lǎoshī:	Duì, zhè shì Měiguó, zhè shì Zhōngguó.
	Hán Jiāng:	Zhōngjiān shì shénme?
	Wáng Zǐxīn:	Shì Tàipíngyáng, nǐmen kàn, wǒ jiā zài Tàipíngyáng shàng! Zài zhèr, Xiàwēiyí!
	Mǎ Lǎoshī:	Duì, Xiàwēiyí zài Tàipíngyáng shàng.

⊙	Cindy:	What about Huang Shan? Where is Huang Shan?
	John:	This I know! Huang Shan is here.

⊙	Teacher Ma:	Where is the United States?
	David:	The United States is here.
	Teacher Ma:	Right, this is the U.S. This is China.
	John:	What's in the middle?
	Cindy:	It's the Pacific Ocean. Look, my home is in the Pacific Ocean! Here, Hawaii!
	Teacher Ma:	Right, Hawaii is in the Pacific Ocean.

王子欣：大伟，美国在哪儿？

陆大伟：是在这儿吗？

韩　江：不对，是在北边。

陆大伟：北边，北边，是在这儿吗？

韩　江：对，那是美国。

王子欣：大伟，你的鼻子在哪儿？

陆大伟：什么？我的鼻子在哪儿？我的鼻子在这儿。

王子欣：不对！不对！

韩　江：你看，陆大伟的鼻子在这儿，在美国北边！

Wáng Zǐxīn: Dàwěi, Měiguó zài nǎr?
Lù Dàwěi: Shì zài zhèr ma?
Hán Jiāng: Bú duì, shì zài běibiān.
Lù Dàwěi: Běibiān, běibiān, shì zài zhèr ma?
Hán Jiāng: Duì, nà shì Měiguó.

Wáng Zǐxīn: Dàwěi, nǐ de bízi zài nǎr?
Lù Dàwěi: Shénme? Wǒ de bízi zài nǎr? Wǒ de bízi zài zhèr.
Wáng Zǐxīn: Bú duì! Bú duì!
Hán Jiāng: Nǐ kàn, Lù Dàwěi de bízi zài zhèr, zài Měiguó běibiān!

Cindy: David, where is the United States?
David: Is it here?
John: No, it's on the northern side.
David: Northern side, northern side ... is it here?
John: Yes, that's the United States.

Cindy: David, where is your nose?
David: What? Where's my nose? My nose is here.
Cindy: Wrong! Wrong!
John: Look, David's nose is here, in the north of the U.S.

二、词语表

1. 课	kè	lesson; class
2. 地理	dìlǐ	geography
3. 教室	jiàoshì	classroom
4. 在	zài	be at or in someplace
5. 哪儿	nǎr	where
6. 二楼	èrlóu	the second floor
7. 第一	dìyī	the first
8. 谢谢	xièxie	thank you
9. 你们	nǐmen	you (pl.)
10. 地图	dìtú	map
11. 北边	běibiān	north
12. 这儿	zhèr	here
13. 美国	Měiguó	U.S.A
14. 中间	zhōngjiān	middle
15. 太平洋	Tàipíngyáng	the Pacific Ocean
16. 上	shàng	(used after a noun) on, in
17. 夏威夷	Xiàwēiyí	Hawaii
18. 鼻子	bízi	nose

三、语言注释

在

In Chinese 在 is used to specify the location of a person, place or thing. If you want to ask where something is located, use "(person/place/thing)+在哪儿". e.g.

A：加拿大（Canada）在哪儿？

B：加拿大在美国北边。

A：台灯在哪儿？

B：台灯在桌子上。

A：王子欣在哪儿？

B：王子欣在家里。

第一

We can use the expression "第+a number" to indicate numerical order. e.g.

第一、第二、第三

But when we count the floors of a building, or count siblings by age, 第 is omitted.

一楼、二楼、三楼

大姐、二姐、三姐

王子欣在二楼。

陆大伟在三楼。

韩江在五楼。

四、汉　字

教 jiào

古文字中，“教”右边是一个人拿着棍子，是教师或父亲在教孩子；左边本身也是一个汉字，意思是仿效，表明受教育者在学习、在按照要求去做。所以，“教”的本义就是教育。这一意义今天也是常用义，如“教室”。

另外，所有的宗教都可以称为“教”，如“基督教、佛教、伊斯兰教”。

In ancient written form, the right half of the character 教 is in the shape of a person holding a stick representing a teacher or a father teaching a child while the left half of the character, itself, is also a character meaning to follow the example of or imitate. This shows that someone receiving education is learning according to certain requirements. Thus, 教 originally means to educate or teach and this is still the commonly used meaning for the character today, as in 教室 (classroom) .

In addition, religions can be referred to as 教 in Chinese such as: 基督教（Christianity), 佛教（Buddhism）, and 伊斯兰教（Islam）.

北 běi

古文字中，“北”象二人相背之形。本义就是相违背，引申指人的脊背。这两个意义见于古代文献，今天已经不用了。“北”用于这两个意义时读bèi 。

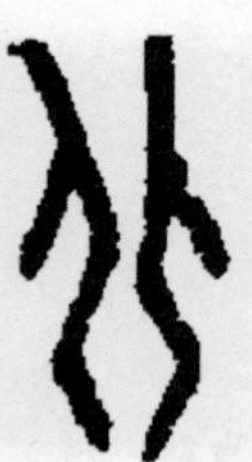

古时候，中国北方的建筑大多是背北向南，因而“北”又引申为表示方位的北方之北，读běi。这一意义在古今都是常用意义。

In ancient script, 北 resembles the shape of two people with their backs to one another. Its original meaning, to go against one another, was extended to mean the back of a person. These two meanings of the character can be found in ancient writings but are no longer used today. When used to express these two meanings the character 北 is pronounced bèi.

In ancient times, the front of most buildings in North China faced south and the back faced north so that the meaning of 北 was extended to indicate the direction north which is pronounced běi. This meaning of the character has been commonly used from the past to the present.

美 měi

古文字中，“美”分别象人头上插着羽毛或加了羊头作装饰之形，古人认为这样很好看，以此为美。中国京剧中，武将头上常常戴着雉鸡翎，显得威武而漂亮；今天世界上仍然有一些民族喜欢佩戴羽毛作装饰。

“美”本义就是漂亮、好看，如“美人、美貌、美丽”。

In ancient Chinese, 美 resembles the shape of a goat's head or of feathers placed on a person's head as a form of decoration. The ancient Chinese felt that this was very attractive and looked upon it as being beautiful. In Peking Opera, military generals often wear two long tail feathers of a pheasant on their heads to appear handsome and mighty. Even today, there are still some ethnic groups in the world that like to wear feathers as a form of headdress.

The original meaning of 美 is beautiful or attractive as in the following: 美人（beautiful woman; belle; beauty (a person)），美貌（beautiful appearance; good looks），and 美丽（beautiful (person or thing)）.

夏 xià

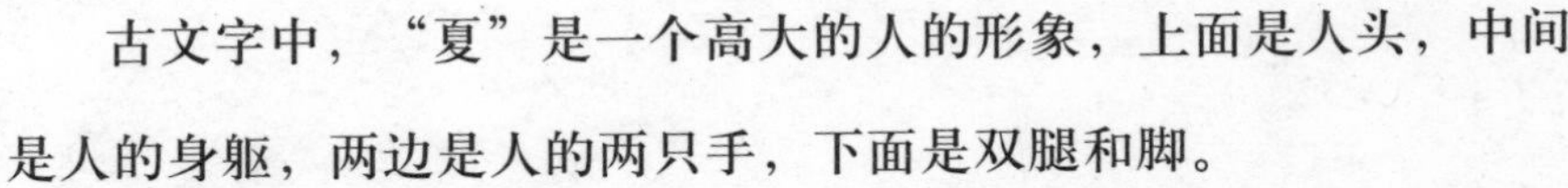

古文字中，“夏”是一个高大的人的形象，上面是人头，中间是人的身躯，两边是人的两只手，下面是双腿和脚。

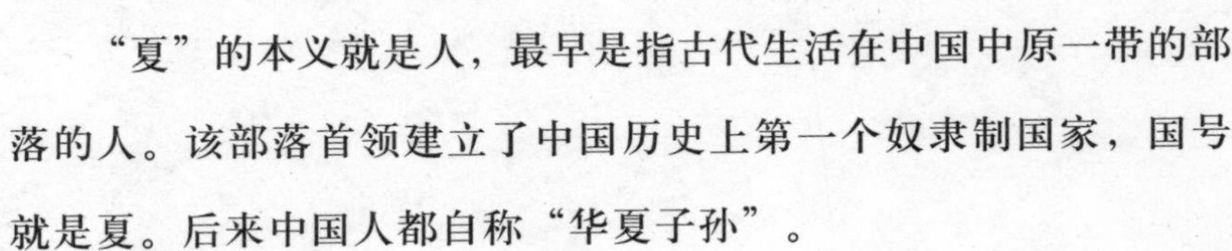

“夏”的本义就是人，最早是指古代生活在中国中原一带的部落的人。该部落首领建立了中国历史上第一个奴隶制国家，国号就是夏。后来中国人都自称“华夏子孙”。

另外，一年四季中的第二个季节也称“夏”，即夏季。

In ancient Chinese script 夏 resembles the image of a large, tall person. The top part of the character is a head, the middle section is a human torso, on either side are two hands, and on the bottom there are two legs and feet. The original meaning of 夏 was man. In its earliest usage, it referred to tribal people living in China's central plains area in ancient times. Their tribal leader established a slave-based society, which became the first dynasty in Chinese history. This nation was called Xia. Later, Chinese called themselves the "descendants of Huaxia (China)".

In addition to the above, the second of the four seasons in a year is also called 夏 or 夏季 (summer).

中国地理 Geography of China

中国位于亚洲东部、太平洋西岸。陆地面积960万平方千米，领土东西跨越约5000千米，南北约5500千米。濒临的海洋有渤海、黄海、东海和南海。沿海分布着5000多个岛屿，台湾岛是第一大岛。中国地势西高东低，呈阶梯状，有山岭、高原、平原、盆地和丘陵，还有许多湖泊和河流。长江是中国第一大河，黄河次之。

▶ **相关信息**

中国的行政区划基本上分为三级：第一级包括省、自治区、直辖市、特别行政区；第二级包括县、自治县、旗、省辖市；第三级包括乡、民族乡、区、镇。总计34个省级行政单位，其中有23个省，5个自治区，北京、上海、天津、重庆4个直辖市，香港、澳门2个特别行政区。

China is located in the eastern part of Asia on the west coast of the Pacific Ocean and covers a land area of 9.6 million square kilometers. The territory spans approximately 5000 kilometers from east to west and 5500 kilometers from north to south. Along the coast of China' s mainland there are four seas, i.e. the Bohai Sea, the Yellow Sea, the East China Sea and the South China Sea. More than 5000 islands are scattered across China' s vast territorial seas, the largest being Taiwan. China' s topography is high in the west and low in the east. It slopes down in the form of a staircase, with mountain ranges, highlands, hilly lands, plains and basins making up different levels. There are also many lakes and rivers. The Yangtze River is the longest river in China and the Yellow River is ranked the second.

▶ **[Additional Notes]**

In China there are three levels of administrative divisions. The first level includes provinces, autonomous regions, municipalities directly under the Central Government, and special administrative regions. The second is divided into autonomous prefectures, counties, autonomous counties and cities directly under the provincial government. The lowest administrative units are townships, ethnic townships, districts and towns. Altogether there are 34 provincial administrative units including 23 provinces, 5 autonomous regions, 4 municipalities directly under the Central Government (Beijing, Shanghai, Tianjin, and Chongqing) and 2 special administrative regions (Hong Kong and Macau).

中学课程设置 High School Curriculums

中学课程主要包括思想品德、语文、数学、外语、科学（或物理、化学、生物）、历史与社会（或历史、地理）、体育与健康、艺术（或音乐、美术）。此外，还有选修课程、技术类课程和综合实践活动等。初级中学设置综合与分科相结合的课程，高中阶段则以分科课程为主。

地理课是中学生的必修课程之一，通常包括地理知识、世界地理和中国地理等内容。

The main courses in Chinese high schools include ethics, Chinese, mathematics, foreign languages, science (covering physics, chemistry and biology), history and social science (covering history and geography), physical education and health, and art (covering music and painting). In addition, there are other practical and comprehensive elective courses and extra-curricular activities. Junior-high schools combine comprehensive courses (such as science, art) with traditional subjects (like history, geography). Senior-high schools, however, focus on the latter.

As a compulsory course in high schools, geography usually covers basic knowledge of geography, world geography and China' s geography.

“贴鼻子”游戏 The Game of “Stick the Nose”

中国孩子经常玩的一种集体游戏。大家先画一张脸，然后其中一个人站在距离这张图片3米左右的位置，蒙住眼睛，手里拿着“鼻子”，摸索着走到图片面前，把“鼻子”贴到“脸上”。由于经常贴错“鼻子”的位置，容易闹笑话，所以比较好玩儿。中国学生常玩的游戏还有：捉迷藏，老鹰抓小鸡，丢手绢等。

Chinese children love playing group games. One of these is “stick the nose”. The children take a piece of paper and draw a face on it. Then one of them stands about 3 meters away, covering his eyes and holding a “nose” in his hand. He then stumbles towards the front of the picture and tries to stick the nose on in the correct place. Because he can' t see, it is very funny as he will usually make a mistake and stick it in the wrong place. Other games that Chinese children enjoy include “Hide and Seek”, “Eagle Catches the Chicken”, “Throw the Handkerchief”, etc.

六、场景探索

场景一

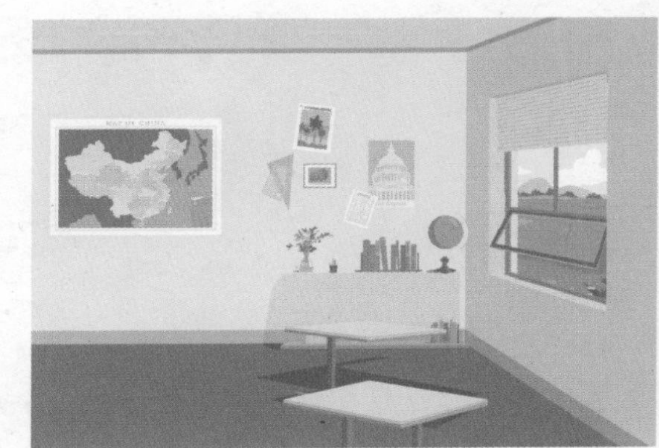

1．窗户 chuānghu window
2．窗帘 chuānglián curtain
3．书架 shūjià bookshelf
4．地图 dìtú map
5．尺子 chǐzi ruler
6．花 huā flower
7．花瓶 huāpíng vase
8．笔筒 bǐtǒng pen container
9．地球仪 dìqiúyí globe
10．书 shū book
11．桌子 zhuōzi desk
12．图片 túpiàn picture

场景二

1．路 lù road
2．路牌 lùpái road sign
3．路灯 lùdēng road lamp
4．树 shù tree
5．房子 fángzi house
6．篱笆 líba fence
7．草地 cǎodì grassy area
8．草 cǎo grass

第七集

你要买什么

第七集　你要买什么

一、课　文

陆大伟：喂，子欣吗？我是大伟。

王子欣：大伟，你好！

陆大伟：我和韩江要去买东西，你去吗？

王子欣：好的，我们一起去。

王子欣：韩江，你要买什么？

韩　江：我买薯片，我特别喜欢薯片。

陆大伟：韩江一天要吃三包薯片！

王子欣：大伟，你呢？

陆大伟：我买可乐，我特别喜欢可乐。

韩　江：大伟一天要喝四瓶可乐！你……

王子欣：我，我一天要吃五个冰淇淋！

Lù Dàwěi: Wéi, Zǐxīn ma? Wǒ shì Dàwěi.

Wáng Zǐxīn: Dàwěi, nǐ hǎo!

Lù Dàwěi: Wǒ hé Hán Jiāng yào qù mǎi dōngxi, nǐ qù ma?

Wáng Zǐxīn: Hǎo de, wǒmen yìqǐ qù.

Wáng Zǐxīn: Hán Jiāng, nǐ yào mǎi shénme?

Hán Jiāng: Wǒ mǎi shǔpiàn, wǒ tèbié xǐhuan chī shǔpiàn.

Lù Dàwěi: Hán Jiāng yì tiān yào chī sān bāo shǔpiàn!

Wáng Zǐxīn: Dàwěi, nǐ ne?

Lù Dàwěi: Wǒ mǎi kělè, wǒ tèbié xǐhuan kělè.

Hán Jiāng: Dàwěi yì tiān yào hē sì píng kělè! Nǐ……

Wáng Zǐxīn: Wǒ, wǒ yì tiān yào chī wǔ gè bīngqílín!

David: Hello, Cindy? This is David.

Cindy: Hello, David!

David: John Hanks and I are going to go shopping. Are you coming?

Cindy: OK, let's go together.

Cindy: John, what are you going to buy?

John: I'm going to buy some potato chips. I really love chips.

David: John eats three bags of chips a day!

Cindy: And you, David?

David: I'm going to buy some coke. I really love coke.

John: David drinks four bottles of coke every day. And you ...

Cindy: Me, I eat five cones of ice-cream a day!

⊙ 韩　江：我还要买光盘。

王子欣：什么光盘？

韩　江：音乐光盘。

王子欣：什么音乐？

韩　江：中国音乐！我喜欢二胡。

王子欣：你买这个吧，特别有名。

韩　江：《二——泉——映——月》，好的，我买这个。

⊙ 陆大伟：你要买篮球？

韩　江：你们看，我像姚明吗？

陆大伟：像，真像！

王子欣：像，特别像！

韩　江：但是，姚明不像我！

⊙ Hán Jiāng: Wǒ hái yào mǎi guāngpán.

Wáng Zǐxīn: Shénme guāngpán?

Hán Jiāng: Yīnyuè guāngpán.

Wáng Zǐxīn: Shénme yīnyuè?

Hán Jiāng: Zhōngguó yīnyuè! Wǒ xǐhuan èrhú.

Wáng Zǐxīn: Nǐ mǎi zhège ba, tèbié yǒumíng.

Hán Jiāng: Èr quán yìng yuè, hǎo de, wǒ mǎi zhège.

⊙ Lù Dàwěi: Nǐ yào mǎi lánqiú?

Hán Jiāng: Nǐmen kàn, wǒ xiàng Yáo Míng ma?

Lù Dàwěi: Xiàng, zhēn xiàng!

Wáng Zǐxīn: Xiàng, tèbié xiàng!

Hán Jiāng: Dànshì, Yáo Míng bú xiàng wǒ!

⊙ John: I also want to buy some CDs.

Cindy: What kind of CDs?

John: Music CDs.

Cindy: What kind of music?

John: Chinese music! I like erhu.

Cindy: You should buy this one then. It's very famous.

John: "Er—Quan—Ying—Yue". Okay, I'll buy this one.

⊙ David: You want to buy a basketball?

John: Watch this, guys. Do I look like Yao Ming?

David: Yeah, you look just like him!

Cindy: Yeah, just like him!

John: But Yao Ming doesn't look like me!

⊙ 王子欣：你们看，真漂亮！我要买一顶。

陆大伟：明天是夏令营最后一天，我也要买一顶。

韩　江：真漂亮！你们看，我像子欣吗？

陆大伟：像，真像！

王子欣：像，特别像！

韩　江：但是……

⊙ 韩　江：我要吃薯片。哎，薯片呢，薯片在哪儿？

陆大伟：我要喝可乐。哎，可乐呢，可乐在哪儿？

王子欣：我要吃冰淇淋。哎，冰淇淋呢，冰淇淋在哪儿？

一　起：在商店里！

⊙ Wáng Zǐxīn: Nǐmen kàn, zhēn piàoliang! Wǒ yào mǎi yì dǐng.

Lù Dàwěi: Míngtiān shì xiàlìngyíng zuìhòu yì tiān, wǒ yě yào mǎi yì dǐng.

Hán Jiāng: Zhēn piàoliang! Nǐmen kàn, wǒ xiàng Zǐxīn ma?

Lù Dàwěi: Xiàng, zhēn xiàng!

Wáng Zǐxīn: Xiàng, tèbié xiàng!

Hán Jiāng: Dànshì……

⊙ Hán Jiāng: Wǒ yào chī shǔpiàn. Éi, shǔpiàn ne, shǔpiàn zài nǎr?

Lù Dàwěi: Wǒ yào hē kělè. Éi, kělè ne, kèlè zài nǎr?

Wáng Zǐxīn: Wǒ yào chī bīngqílín. Éi, bīngqílín ne, bīngqílín zài nǎr?

Yìqǐ: Zài shāngdiàn li!

⊙ Cindy: Look, it's so beautiful! I want to buy one.

David: Tomorrow is the last day of the language camp. I want to buy a hat too.

John: It's so beautiful! Look, guys, do I look like Cindy?

David: Yeah, just like her!

Cindy: Yeah, we're definitely alike!

John: But...

⊙ John: I want to eat some potato chips. Eh?! The Chips! Where are the potato chips?

David: I want to drink some coke. Eh?! Coke, where is my coke?

Cindy: I want to eat an ice-cream. Eh?! Ice-cream, where is my ice-cream?

Together: In the store!

二、词语表

1. 和	hé	and; with
2. 要	yào	to be going to; to want
3. 去	qù	to go
4. 买	mǎi	to buy
5. 好的	hǎode	OK; fine
6. 一起	yìqǐ	together
7. 薯片	shǔpiàn	potato chips
8. 特别	tèbié	especially
9. 天	tiān	day
10. 吃	chī	to eat
11. 包	bāo	bag; package; parcel
12. 喝	hē	to drink
13. 瓶	píng	bottle
14. 可乐	kělè	coke
15. 冰淇淋	bīngqílín	ice cream

16. 光盘	guāngpán	CD
17. 篮球	lánqiú	basketball
18. 像	xiàng	to be like; to resemble
19. 顶	dǐng	a measure word for things which have a top
20. 哎	éi	interjection (used to show surprise or disapproval)
21. 商店	shāngdiàn	store; shop
22. 喂*	wéi	interjection (used as hello in answering the telephone)
23. 吧*	ba	particle (indicating a suggestion)
24. 二泉映月*	èrquányìngyuè	Er Quan Ying Yue, a famous Chinese erhu solo
25. 明天*	míngtiān	tomorrow
26. 夏令营*	xiàlìngyíng	summer camp
27. 最后*	zuìhòu	the last

The symbol * indicates that the corresponding word is not practiced in this episode.

三、语言注释

要

You can use 要（want to）before a verb to express intention or desire. For example:

我要买薯片。

我要去美国。

王子欣要去中国。

陆大伟要喝可乐。

什么

You can use 什么 before another noun to ask for more information about it. Look at the following:

这是什么书？

这是汉语书。

A：这是什么画？

B：这是山水画。

A：这是什么光盘？

B：这是音乐光盘。

四、汉 字

天 tiān

古文字中，“天”下面象人的形状，上面是人的头。“天”的本义就是人的头顶或者头顶之上的天空。“天”的天空义今天还在使用，如“天上有很多云”。

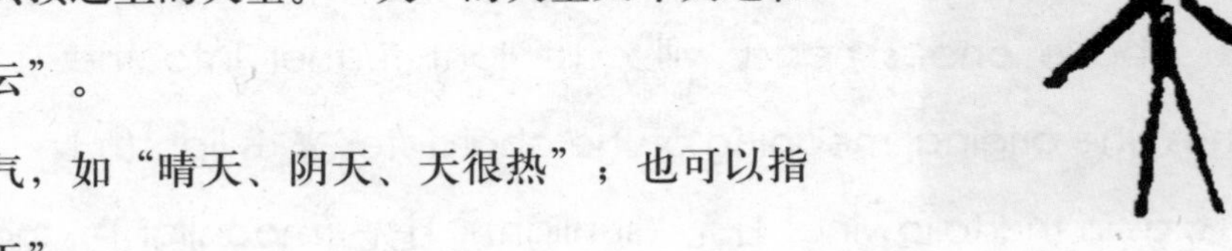

“天”还可以指天气，如“晴天、阴天、天很热”；也可以指白天，如“明天、第二天”。

In ancient script, the lower part of 天 resembles a person while the upper part resembles a head. The original meaning of 天 is the crown of the head or the sky above one’s head. Its meaning of sky is still in use today, as in 天上有很多云 (There are a lot of clouds in the sky.). The character 天 can also be used to refer to weather, as in: 晴天 (sunny day), 阴天 (cloudy day), and 天很热 (the weather’s very hot). This character can also mean day, as in 明天 (tomorrow), 第二天 (the next/second/following day).

包 bāo

古文字中，“包”象尚未长成的孩子被包裹在胎衣中之形。

“包”可用作动词，意思是用纸、布等把东西裹起来，如“包书、包饺子”；也可指装东西用的袋子，如“书包、钱包”。

In ancient Chinese script, 包 resembles the shape of an as yet fully-formed fetus enveloped in the placenta. 包 can be used as a verb and, in this sense, it means to use paper, cloth, or other materials to wrap up something. Examples of this include: 包书 (wrap up a book in paper; put a jacket on a book) and 包饺子 (wrap dumplings). It can also be used to refer to a bag or pouch to put things in, as in: 书包 (schoolbag) or 钱包 (wallet).

光 guāng

古文字中，“光”上面是火，下面是人，把火举在头上，火光便可以照得更远。“光”字的本义就是光明，如“日光、月光、灯光”。

In ancient written form, the upper half of the character 光 represents “fire” and the lower half represents “man”. Lifting up a flame above one’s head will cast light further into the distance. Thus, the original meaning of the character 光 is light(n.) or brightness, as in the following: 日光 (sunlight), 月光 (moonlight), and 灯光 (lamplight).

美式快餐在中国　American Fast Foods in China

在中国，常见的美式快餐有汉堡、热狗、炸鸡、薯片、沙拉、三明治等。肯德基和麦当劳在中国的一些大中城市开设了大量的分店。在其消费人群中，少男少女和由父母陪伴的小孩占有较大的比例。为了适应中国人的口味，肯德基还陆续推出了一些传统的中餐，如"老北京鸡肉卷"、"寒稻香蘑饭"、"香菇鸡肉粥"、"海鲜蔬菜汤"等。

相关信息

在中国的美式快餐店大多开在都市繁华地段而不是在汽车站或加油站。多数中国人是从欣赏异国文化的角度品味美式快餐。人们往往边吃边喝，轻松地欣赏街景，较难见到美国快餐店应有的紧张气氛。

The most common American fast foods in China are hamburgers, hotdogs, fried chicken, potato chips, salad and sandwiches. The major distributors of these are KFC and McDonald' s that have established a great number of branches throughout the larger cities in China. Teenagers and children with their parents are their main consumers. In order to suit the taste of Chinese people, KFC has successively brought out some traditional Chinese foods like "Old Beijing Chicken Roll", "Cold Wheat Mushroom Rice", "Mushroom Chicken Porridge" and "Seafood Vegetable Soup".

[Additional Notes]

US fast food restaurants in China are usually opened in the commercial center of the city but not at bus or gas stations. Most Chinese people enjoy US fast food from the perspective of appreciating an exotic culture. In most cases, customers can leisurely enjoy the view of the street while eating as the atmosphere in these restaurants is usually relaxed and laid-back.

购物场所 Places for Shopping

中国的购物场所包括商场、超市、自由市场等等。商场是综合性的购物场所，商品种类齐全，一些大型商场汇集了来自世界各地的产品。有的商场集购物、餐饮、娱乐于一体，可以满足消费者多方面、多层次的需求。在商场购物，一般不能还价，但是服装常常在季末或节日期间打折。超市是买日常用品的好去处，除了“物美”、“华联”等中国连锁超市外，“沃尔玛”（Wal-Mart）、“家乐福（Carrefour）”等已经进入中国。随着电脑的普及，网上超市正不断涌现。很多外国朋友也非常喜欢去中国的自由市场，因为在那里买东西可以讨价还价，他们认为这是一种有趣的经历。

Places for shopping in China include department stores, supermarkets, private businesses and open-air markets. Department stores are comprehensive shopping centers, providing goods of almost all types. In some big stores, products are gathered from all over the world. Some combine shopping with food and entertainment so as to meet the demands of all different consumers. Bargaining is not usually possible when shopping in big stores but many products, like clothes, go on sale at between seasons and during holidays and festivals. Supermarkets are a good place to buy daily necessities. Besides some Chinese supermarket chains like Wumei and Hualian, Wal-Mart and Carrefour are also common in larger cities. With the popularization of computers, online shopping is also becoming more and more popular. Many foreigners are also fond of China's open-air markets where they can bargain freely, which, for them, is an interesting experience.

二泉映月 The Moon Reflected on the Second Spring

“二泉映月”是民间音乐家阿炳于20世纪30年代末创作的二胡曲，表现了压抑悲怆的情调和倔强不屈的性格，具有强烈的感染力。曲名中的“二泉”指江苏无锡的惠山泉，被誉为“天下第二泉”。

相关信息

阿炳（1893—1950），本名华彦钧，江苏无锡惠山人。民间音乐家，后双目失明，人称“瞎子阿炳”。二胡曲“二泉映月”由他本人演奏并经录音整理后，又出现多种形式的改编曲，如器乐合奏曲、弦乐四重奏和钢琴曲等等。

“The Moon Reflected on the Second Spring” is a piece played on the Erhu composed by Ah Bing, a blind musician, during the late 1930s. It is an impressive piece, reflecting depression and determination. The “second spring” mentioned in the title refers to the Huishan Spring in Wuxi, Jiangsu Province, where Ah Bing lived. This spring is crowned as the second most beautiful in China.

[Additional Notes]

Ah Bing (1893-1950), originally named Hua Yanjun, was born in Huishan, Wuxi in Jiangsu Province. He was a folk musician, affectionately called Blind Ah Bing, because he went blind in his later years. The Erhu piece “The Moon Reflected on the Second Spring” was played and recorded by Ah Bing himself and was later adapted to the instrumental ensemble, string quartet and piano, etc.

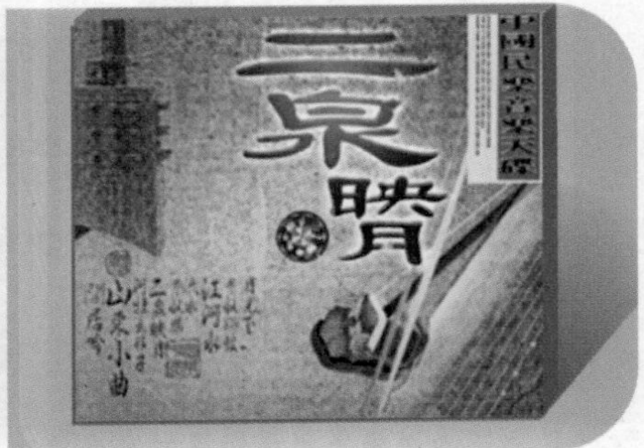

六、场景探索

场景一

1．橄榄球　gǎnlǎnqiú　rugby ball

2．足球　zúqiú　soccer

3．篮球　lánqiú　basketball

4．羽毛球　yǔmáoqiú　shuttlecock

5．乒乓球　pīngpāngqiú　ping-pong ball

6．网球　wǎngqiú　tennis ball

7．排球　páiqiú　volleyball

8．乒乓球拍　pīngpāngqiúpāi　table tennis bat

9．羽毛球拍　yǔmáoqiúpāi　racket

10．网球拍　wǎngqiúpāi　tennis racket

11．运动鞋　yùndòngxié　sport footwear

12．冰鞋　bīngxié　skating boots

13．哑铃　yǎlíng　dumbbell

14．滑板　huábǎn　skateboard

15．跳绳　tiàoshéng　skipping rope

16．帽子　màozi　cap

场景二

1. 苹果	píngguǒ	apple
2. 香蕉	xiāngjiāo	banana
3. 西瓜	xīguā	watermelon
4. 梨	lí	pear
5. 葡萄	pútao	grape
6. 牛奶	niúnǎi	milk
7. 果汁	guǒzhī	fruit juice
8. 薯片	shǔpiàn	potato chips
9. 雪碧	xuěbì	Sprite
10. 纯净水	chúnjìngshuǐ	purified water
11. 绿茶	lǜchá	green tea
12. 啤酒	píjiǔ	beer
13. 可乐	kělè	coke

第八集

夏令营最后一天

第八集　夏令营最后一天

一、课 文

王子欣：大伟，今天几号？

陆大伟：二十七号，今天是夏令营最后一天。

韩　江：我要去买花。

陆大伟：我们一起去。

王子欣：送给我吗？

陆大伟：对，送给你，也送给马老师！

陆大伟：马老师，这是我们送给你的花。

马老师：真漂亮，谢谢你们！我也有东西送给你们。

韩　江：这是什么？

王子欣：我知道，这是中国，中国……，中国花！

Wáng Zǐxīn: Dàwěi, jīntiān jǐ hào?

Lù Dàwěi: Èrshíqī hào, jīntiān shì xiàlìngyíng zuìhòu yì tiān.

Hán Jiāng: Wǒ yào qù mǎi huā .

Lù Dàwěi: Wǒmen yìqǐ qù.

Wáng Zǐxīn: Sòng gěi wǒ ma?

Lù Dàwěi: Duì, sòng gěi nǐ, yě sòng gěi Mǎ lǎoshī!

Lù Dàwěi: Mǎ lǎoshī, zhè shì wǒmen sòng gěi nǐ de huā.

Mǎ Lǎoshī: Zhēn piàoliang, xièxie nǐmen! Wǒ yě yǒu dōngxi sòng gěi nǐmen.

Hán Jiāng: Zhè shì shénme?

Wáng Zǐxīn: Wǒ zhīdào, zhè shì Zhōngguó, Zhōngguó……Zhōngguóhuā!

Cindy: David, what's the date today?

David: Today is the 27th, the last day of the language camp.

John: I want to buy some flowers.

David: Let's go together.

Cindy: For me?

David: Yes, for you, and also for Teacher Ma.

David: Teacher Ma, these are some flowers we bought for you.

Teacher Ma: So beautiful, thank you! I've got something for you guys too.

John: What is this?

Cindy: I know, this is a Chinese, Chinese... Chinese flower!

⊙ 马老师：　这不是中国花，这是中国结。

王子欣：　对对对，是中国结。

陆大伟：　啊，中国结，真漂亮！

韩　江：　对，特别可爱。谢谢马老师！

⊙ 陆大伟：　马老师，上海在这儿，对吗？

马老师：　对。你们知道吗？我家在上海。

陆大伟：　你家在上海，所以你要回上海。

马老师：　对。

陆大伟：　马老师，你家有几口人？

马老师：　我家有四口人，爸爸、妈妈、我，还有一个弟弟。

Mǎ Lǎoshī: Zhè bú shì Zhōngguóhuā, zhè shì Zhōngguójié.

Wáng Zǐxīn: Duì duì duì, shì Zhōngguójié.

Lù Dàwěi: À, Zhōngguójié, zhēn piàoliang!

Hán Jiāng: Duì, tèbié kě'ài. Xièxie Mǎ lǎoshī!

Lù Dàwěi: Mǎ lǎoshī, Shànghǎi zài zhèr, duì ma?

Mǎ Lǎoshī: Duì. Nǐmen zhīdào ma? Wǒ jiā zài Shànghǎi.

Lù Dàwěi: Nǐ jiā zài Shànghǎi, suǒyǐ nǐ yào huí Shànghǎi.

Mǎ Lǎoshī: Duì.

Lù Dàwěi: Mǎ lǎoshī, Nǐ jiā yǒu jǐ kǒu rén?

Mǎ Lǎoshī: Wǒ jiā yǒu sì kǒu rén, bàba, māma, wǒ, hái yǒu yí gè dìdi.

Teacher Ma: This isn't a Chinese flower. It's a Chinese knot.

Cindy: Right, right. It's a Chinese knot.

David: Ah, a Chinese knot, it's so beautiful!

John: Yes, it's really cute. Thank you, Teacher Ma.

David: Teacher Ma, Shanghai is here, right?

Teacher Ma: Right. Did you know that my home is in Shanghai?

David: Your home is in Shanghai, so you will return to Shanghai.

Teacher Ma: Right.

David: Teacher Ma, how many people are there in your family?

Teacher Ma: There are four people in my family, Dad, Mom, I and my younger brother.

⊙ 王子欣：马老师几号回上海？

马老师：我三十号回上海。大伟，你呢？几号去北京？

陆大伟：啊，我明天去北京。

⊙ 王子欣：马老师，我们一起合影，好吗？

马老师：好的。

韩　江：我也要和马老师合影！

陆大伟：我们四个人一起！

王子欣：谁帮我们拍照呢？

韩　江：看，罗斯！

陆大伟：罗斯，你帮我们拍照，好吗？

罗　斯：好的！大家一起说“茄——子”！

众　声：“茄——子”！

⊙ Wáng Zǐxīn: Mǎ lǎoshī jǐ hào huí Shànghǎi?

Mǎ Lǎoshī: Wǒ sānshí hào huí Shànghǎi. Dàwěi, nǐ ne? Jǐ hào qù Běijīng?

Lù Dàwěi: À, wǒ míngtiān qù Běijīng.

⊙ Wáng Zǐxīn: Mǎ lǎoshī, wǒmen yìqǐ héyǐng, hǎo ma?

Mǎ Lǎoshī: Hǎo de.

Hán Jiāng: Wǒ yě yào hé Mǎ lǎoshī héyǐng!

Lù Dàwěi: Wǒmen sì gè rén yìqǐ!

Wáng Zǐxīn: Shuí bāng wǒmen pāizhào ne?

Hán Jiāng: Kàn, Luósī!

Lù Dàwěi: Luósī, nǐ bāng wǒmen pāizhào, hǎo ma?

Luósī: Hǎo de! Dàjiā yìqǐ shuō “qié—zi”!

Zhòng shēng: “Qié—zi”!

⊙ Cindy: When will you return to Shanghai, Teacher Ma?

Teacher Ma: I will return to Shanghai on the 30th. David, when will you go to Beijing?

David: Ah, I will go to Beijing tomorrow.

⊙ Cindy: Teacher Ma, can we take a photo together?

Teacher Ma: Okay.

John: I want to take a picture with Teacher Ma, too.

David: Let's take a picture of the four of us together!

Cindy: Who'll help us take the picture then?

John: Look, Ross!

David: Ross, take a picture for us, Okay?

Ross: Okay! Everyone all together now, “Qie...zi”!

All: “Qie...zi”!

二、词语表

1. 今天	jīntiān	today
2. 号	hào	date; number
3. 二十七	èrshíqī	twenty seven
4. 夏令营	xiàlìngyíng	summer camp
5. 最后	zuìhòu	the last
6. 花	huā	flower
7. 送给	sònggěi	to send to
8. 中国结	zhōngguójié	Chinese knot
9. 上海	Shànghǎi	Shanghai
10. 所以	suǒyǐ	so; therefore; as a result
11. 回	huí	to return
12. 三十	sānshí	thirty
13. 北京	Běijīng	Beijing
14. 明天	míngtiān	tomorrow
15. 合影	héyǐng	to take a group photo
16. 帮	bāng	to help
17. 拍照	pāizhào	to take photos
18. 说	shuō	to say; to speak
19. 茄子	qiézi	eggplant

三、语言注释

今天几号？

If you want to ask "what's the date today?" you can say 今天几号？号 can also be used before a number to tell the date. Note: It is not necessary to use 是 when asking or telling someone the date. e. g.

A：今天几号？ B：今天二十七号。

A：明天几号？ B：明天二十八号。

A：今天几号？

B：今天二十五号，今天是圣诞节（Christmas day）！

呢

呢 can be used at the end of a question which includes question words such as 谁、什么、哪儿、几 etc. Look at the examples below:

谁是孔子呢？

这是谁的书呢？

你叫什么名字呢？

松鼠在哪儿呢？

他家有几口人呢？

A：韩江喜欢薯片，王子欣喜欢什么呢？ B：她喜欢冰淇淋。

好吗？

You can use 好吗 to ask for agreement or as a polite form of asking for help. e.g.

我们一起合影，好吗？

你帮我们拍照，好吗？

A：我们买一个中国结，好吗？

B：好。

A：你要去旅行吗？

B：对，我要去旅行。

A：我们一起去，好吗？

B：好。

令 lìng

古文字中，“令”上面是一个木铎，古代人发号令的时候常常摇着木铎；下面是一个跪着的人，表示正在接受命令。“令”的本义就是发号令、下命令，也可以指发号施令的人或者发出的命令，如“法令、军令”。

另外，“令”还有时节、季节的意思，如“夏令、冬令”。

In ancient script, the top half of 令 is a large wooden bell. In ancient times, people would often swing large wooden bells to signal military commands. The bottom half of the character is a man kneeling down, which signifies that he is receiving orders. The original meaning of 令 is to send signals and orders or give commands. It can also refer either to a person who issues orders or to the orders issued themselves, for example: 法令（decree）and 军令（military order).

In addition, 令 may denote a period of time or season of the year, as with the following: 夏令（summer; summer weather）and 冬令（winter; winter weather).

回 huí

古文字中，“回”象曲折环绕之形，本义就是曲折、环绕。“回”在今天有很多意思，都跟它的本义“曲折环绕”有联系：可以指从别的地方到原来的地方，如“回来、回家、回国”；又有掉转的意思，如“回头、回身”；还有答复的意思，如“回信、回电话”。

In ancient script 回 resembles a winding, encircling shape and its original meaning is just that, to wind or encircle. Today 回 has many meanings, all of which are related to its original meaning. Firstly, 回 can mean to return from another place, as in: 回来（come back; return), 回家（return home; go home), 回国（return to/visit your native country). It can also mean to turn around, as in: 回头（turn around; glance back）or 回身（turn round; turn one's body to face the opposite direction). Still another meaning of 回 is to reply, for example: 回信（write back; a letter of reply）and 回电话（return a telephone call).

明 míng

古文字中，“明”左边是太阳，右边是月亮。月亮快要落山、太阳刚刚升起，表示天亮了，有明亮之意。在明亮的地方，什么都能看清楚，所以“明”又有清楚的意思，如“明白、说明”。

“明”还表示顺序在“今”之后的，如“明年、明天、明晚”。

In its ancient written form, the left side of 明 represents the sun while the right side represents the moon. As the moon dips below the mountains and the sun just begins to rise, it heralds daybreak, and thus, 明 denotes light(adj.) or bright. Wherever there is brightness, things may be seen clearly. For this reason, 明 also means clear, as in: 明白 (be clear about; understand; plain; clear) and 说明 (explain; show).

明 also signifies a sequence in time following after 今 (today; this (evening/year)) such as: 明年 (next year), 明天 (tomorrow) and 明晚 (tomorrow evening).

明	明	明	明	明	明	明	明				
天	天	天	天	天							
回	回	回	回	回	回	回					
中	中	中	中	中							
国	国	国	国	国	国	国	国	国			

中国结 Chinese Knot Tying

中国结是一种传统的艺术品，用长长的红、黄、蓝等彩绳，采用多种手法，编成上下一致、左右对称、正反相同、首尾相衔的完整造型。从大型的房间挂饰到小巧的服饰，都可以见到美丽的中国结。除了装饰作用以外，中国结还用来表达良好祝福和美好愿望。

Chinese knot tying is a traditional work of art, which uses long and colorful strings and various knitting skills to create all sorts of patterns and handicrafts. Some are symmetrical from top to bottom, and some from left to right. Others have the same fancy patterns on both sides.

Chinese knots can be used for many different purposes, from big decorations to exquisite clothing accessories. They are used to express blessing and good wishes.

上海 Shanghai

上海，简称“沪”或“申”，是中国最大的经济中心和国际化大都市，也是一座历史悠久的旅游城市，迄今还保留着唐、宋、元、明、清以来的一些古迹和富有特色的园林。现代化的新景观则有东方明珠电视塔、人民广场和外滩上各具特色的中西建筑物。

▶ 相关信息

上海位于中国南北海岸线的中部，交通便利，位置优越，是一个良好的港口。上海属亚热带季风性气候，四季分明，日照充分，雨量充沛，气候温和湿润，春秋较短，冬夏较长。

上海市面积6340.5平方公里。截止2003年，全市人口为1341.8万人。人均国民生产总值位居中国大陆各省级地区之首，对促进中国经济和社会的发展具有举足轻重的作用。

Shanghai, abbreviated as Hu or Shen, is the biggest financial center and international cosmopolitan in China. It is also a tourist city with a long history. Up until now, there are still some remains of ancient relics and gardens from the Tang, Song, Yuan, Ming and Qing Dynasties. Some of Shanghai's modern sites include the Oriental Pearl Tower, the People's Square and the Chinese and Western architectural styles found in the Bund.

[Additional Notes]

Shanghai is located in the center of China's eastern coast. This excellent geographical location makes it a nice harbor and provides convenient transport to and from other parts of China and foreign countries. The city has a subtropical monsoon climate, abundant sunshine and sufficient rainfall. It has four distinct seasons, with short spring and fall and long winter and summer.

Shanghai covers an area of 6340.5 square kilometers. By the end of 2003 the population was estimated to be 13.418 million. With the highest average GNP of all China's provincial administrative units, Shanghai has played a crucial role in promoting the development of Chinese economy and society.

北京 Beijing

北京，简称“京”，是中华人民共和国的首都，中国的政治、文化和国际交往中心。北京已有3000多年的悠久历史，是辽、金、元、明、清五朝古都，也是世界历史文化名城之一。现已开放的文物古迹和游览景点有200多处，主要有故宫、北海、天坛、颐和园、八达岭、十三陵等。

▶ **相关信息**

北京地处华北大平原的北部，东面与天津市毗连，其余均与河北省相邻。北京属暖温带半湿润气候区，四季分明，春秋短促，冬夏较长。

北京市面积16807.8平方公里。截止2003年，全市常住人口1456.4万人。中国的56个民族都有人在北京居住、工作和学习。北京目前已成为一个充满生机与活力、正在向现代化迈进的综合性产业城市。

Beijing, abbreviated as Jing, is the capital of the People's Republic of China, as well as the center of the nation's politics, culture and international exchanges. With a history of more than 3000 years, Beijing has been the capital of the Liao, Jin, Yuan, Ming and Qing dynasties and is one of the world's most historical and cultural cities. Until now, over 200 cultural relics, historical sites and tourist spots have been opened to the public. The main sites are the Palace Museum, Beihai (North Lake) Park, the Temple of Heaven, the Summer Palace, Badaling Great Wall and the Thirteen Tombs of the Ming Emperors.

▶ **[Additional Notes]**

Beijing is located on the northern edge of the North China Plain, with Tianjin City on its eastern border and Hebei Province on the other three sides. It has a continental monsoon climate and four distinct seasons. Spring and autumn are short while winter and summer are long.

The city of Beijing covers an area of 16807.8 square kilometers and has a total of 14.564 million residents by the end of 2003. People from 56 ethnic groups work, live and study in the city. Beijing has now become a modern dynamic metropolis with a wide range of industries.

拍照用语 Words for Taking Pictures

“茄——子”发音时嘴角向两边拉开，口型呈现出微笑的模样，像英语的“cheese”或“whiskey”。拍照时，特别是多人合影时，中国人习惯说“茄子”。

When taking pictures, especially a group photo, the Chinese people often say Qiezi (literally meaning “eggplant”). When pronounced, the word pulls the corners of the mouth to both sides, creating a smiling face in the similar way as the words “cheese” or “whiskey” in English.

时间顺序 Time Order

汉语表达时间的顺序和英语相反，按照从大到小的排列方式，先说年，再说月份，最后说日期，比如2004年2月23日。这反映了中国人从整体到个体、从一般到特殊的整体思维特点。

The order in which time is expressed in Chinese differs from that of English. The Chinese people order time units from the biggest to the smallest, i.e. year, month, date, as in “2004 nián 2 yuè 23 rì”. This reflects the Chinese thought pattern of perceiving things as a whole, from general to specific or from large to small, focusing on the whole rather than the part.

六、场景探索

场景一

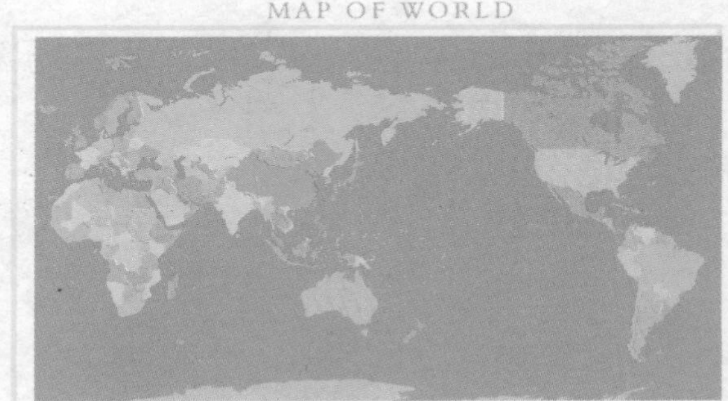

1. 北京 Běijīng Beijing
2. 纽约 Niǔyuē New York
3. 渥太华 Wōtàihuá Ottawa
4. 墨尔本 Mò'ěrběn Melbourne
5. 惠灵顿 Huìlíngdùn Wellington
6. 莫斯科 Mòsīkē Moscow
7. 伦敦 Lúndūn London
8. 巴黎 Bālí Paris
9. 开罗 Kāiluó Cairo
10. 新德里 Xīndélǐ New Delhi
11. 东京 Dōngjīng Tokyo
12. 墨西哥城 Mòxīgēchéng Mexico City
13. 柏林 Bólín Berlin

场景二

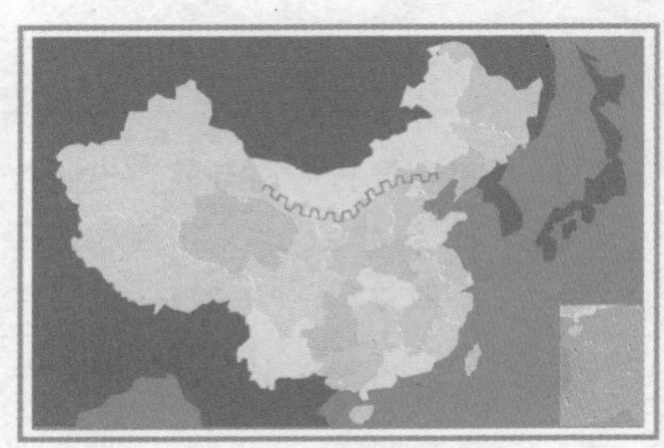

1. 乌鲁木齐 Wūlǔmùqí Urumqi
2. 哈尔滨 Hā'ěrbīn Harbin
3. 拉萨 Lāsà Lhasa
4. 西安 Xī'ān Xi'an
5. 南京 Nánjīng Nanjing
6. 广州 Guǎngzhōu Guangzhou
7. 香港 Xiānggǎng Hong Kong
8. 上海 Shànghǎi Shanghai
9. 长春 Chángchūn Changchun
10. 重庆 Chóngqìng Chongqing
11. 北京 Běijīng Beijing
12. 武汉 Wǔhàn Wuhan

图书在版编目（CIP）数据

乘风汉语学生用书. 1 / 刘颂浩主编. —北京：高等教育出版社，2005.7 (2006 重印)
ISBN 7-04-018210-6

Ⅰ. 乘... Ⅱ. 刘... Ⅲ. 汉语-对外汉语教学-教材 Ⅳ. H195.4

中国版本图书馆 CIP 数据核字 (2005) 第 077665 号

责任编辑 白震坤 梁 宇 封面设计 王凌波 插图选配 华夏大地教育网
版式设计 阳光领域 责任校对 许月萍 责任印制 韩 刚

出版发行 高等教育出版社
社 址 北京市西城区德外大街 4 号
邮政编码 100011
总 机 010-58581000

经 销 蓝色畅想图书发行有限公司
印 刷 北京中科印刷有限公司

购书热线 010-58581118
免费咨询 800-810-0598
网 址 http://www.hep.edu.cn
http://www.hep.com.cn
网上订购 http://www.landraco.com
http://www.landraco.com.cn
畅想教育 http://www.widedu.com

开 本 889×1194 1/16
印 张 8.75
字 数 200 000

版 次 2005 年 7 月第 1 版
印 次 2006 年 7 月第 3 次印刷

物料号 18210-A0

ISBN 7-04-018210-6
04200